1991

THE SAINT AUGUSTINE LECTURE SERIES
Villanova University

Saint Augustine and
the Augustinian Tradition

Robert P. Russell, O.S.A.

EDITOR

Benedict A. Paparella, Ph.D.

ASSOCIATE EDITOR

THE SAINT AUGUSTINE LECTURE 1964

Augustine and
the Greek Philosophers

JOHN F. CALLAHAN

Introduction

The Annual Saint Augustine Lecture was formally inaugurated at Villanova University in the Spring of 1959. Dedicated to the general theme "Saint Augustine and the Augustinian Tradition," this lecture series has presented in successive years outstanding scholars from here and abroad who have explored various facets of Augustine's thought and influence having particular significance and relevance to the intellectual and religious problems of our age.

Dr. John Callahan's competence in the fields of classical and philosophic learning is widely recognized. In Patristic studies he is well known as one of the editors of the critical edition of the works of Gregory of Nyssa, undertaken by the Institute for Classical Studies of Harvard University. Since the publication of his work in 1948 entitled "Four Views of Time in Ancient Philosophy," which included an important chapter on Augustine's analysis of time, Professor Callahan has continued his researches into the thought and text of this great Doctor of the Church with the special emphasis upon Platonic and earlier Christian influences.

In the present work, "Augustine and the Greek Philosophers," Dr. Callahan makes available to us a considerable and significant part of this fruitful scholarship. The original lecture, delivered in the Spring of 1964, has been greatly enriched by the addition of copious and critical notes which will prove an asset for all who wish to pursue further the many rich insights suggested in this remarkable lecture.

Robert P. Russell, O.S.A.
Editor

Villanova University
Villanova, Pennsylvania

Preface

The present work appears here, except for minor alterations, as it was originally written before the lecture itself, for which numerous omissions had to be made for reasons of time. The editors have generously allowed the fuller version to be printed, along with notes that supply, I trust, the basic references required by the text and offer a limited discussion of some pertinent topics. They have also permitted me to use a considerable amount of Greek and Latin in the text and notes, but, in conformity with the nature of the lecture, the text is intended to be intelligible without a knowledge of these languages.

I am especially glad that I was able to include in the notes an important passage in Greek from Gregory of Nyssa; I have referred extensively to his works here, since he seems to me to represent in an outstanding way the Greek philosophical tradition in its Christian guise. The text of this passage, which is taken from my forthcoming volume of two treatises of Gregory, *De oratione dominica* and *De beatitudinibus*, is used with the kind permission of E. J. Brill.

The study involved in this work goes back many years and owes much to periods of time provided by the Rockefeller Foundation, the Fund for the Advancement of Education, the Guggenheim Memorial Foundation, and Georgetown University, to all of which I make grateful acknowledgment. Most of the actual composition was done at the Fondation Hardt, Vandoeuvres-Geneva, which placed its library and other facilities at my disposal; to the Conseil and to the other members of the Fondation who cooperated in the enterprise I give my sincere thanks. Finally, I am grateful to the editors for offering me the opportunity of participating in this series and for seeing the book through the press.

J. F. C.

To Richard McKeon

Contents

Introduction   vii

Preface   ix

I. *The "Ontological" Argument for the Existence of God*

1. Augustine and Anselm   1
2. The Divine Perfection in Greek Thought to Plotinus   5
3. The Divine Perfection in Gregory of Nyssa   11
4. The Divine Perfection in Augustine   16
5. Incorruptibility in Augustine and His Predecessors   20
6. The Greek Background of the "Ontological" Argument   29
7. The "Ontological" Argument in Augustine and Anselm   32
8. The Moral Universe of Augustine   39
9. The "Ontological" Character of Augustine's Argument   43

II. *The Flight of the Soul*

1. The Divine Origin of the Soul in Greek Thought to Plotinus   47
2. The Flight of the Soul in Augustine   52

3. The Flight of the Soul in Gregory of Nyssa   55

4. Development within Augustine's Thought   58

5. Augustine and Gregory of Nyssa Compared   62

6. Distinctive Features of Augustine's Treatment   70

III. *Time and the Soul*

1. The Relation of Time to Soul in Greek Thought to Plotinus   74

2. The Nature of Time in Gregory of Nyssa   77

3. The Psychological Approach of Augustine   82

4. Augustine and His Predecessors Compared   87

5. The Moral Aspect of Time   90

6. Conclusion   93

Notes   96

Index   116

Augustine and
the Greek Philosophers

I. The "Ontological" Argument for the Existence of God

1. Augustine and Anselm

In discussing some of the relationships between Augustine and the Greek philosophical tradition that preceded him it may seem strange to take as one's point of departure an argument that is conceived to be the special contribution of a thinker who lived some seven centuries after him. I refer to the argument, called by the name "ontological" since the time of Kant, proposed in the eleventh century by Anselm to prove the existence of God. This argument has had a long and varied history, and there has been no end to the controversy regarding its validity and even its precise meaning. To look at whatever role Augustine may have had in the formulation of this argument not only may indicate something of the influence of the Augustinian philosophy on later thinkers even to the present day, but, more relevantly to our present purpose, may throw some light on the manner in which Augustine was able to take diverse materials from the Greek philosophers and transmute them into something that was an original creation in its own right and at the same time a source of inspiration for those who came after him.

With this in mind we might glance briefly at Anselm's ontological argument and then see what relation it may have to Augustine. Anselm himself tells us that, having previously formulated a series of arguments, he now sought for a single argument that would be sufficient all by itself to prove the existence of God.[1] The crucial sentences of the argument, which he eventually discovered, run somewhat as follows:

> We believe God to be something than which a greater cannot be thought. Such a being surely cannot exist only in the mind; for then it could be thought of as existing in reality also, which is greater. If then the being than which a greater cannot be thought exists only in the mind, it is a being than which a greater can be thought. Since this is a contradiction, there exists therefore something than which a greater cannot be thought, both in the mind and in reality.[2]

It is not necessary for our purposes to examine the argument in detail, in its metaphysical and epistemological implications, or in what it might actually be said to prove; and it would be still less to the point to look into the attitudes adopted by later thinkers towards it. On this occasion I am interested rather in whatever origins may be found for this type of argumentation in Augustine and in his predecessors. The search—and a very natural search it is—for an Augustinian source of the ontological argument of Anselm has already led to the work *On Christian doctrine,* where one sentence in particular has seemed to find an echo in the words of Anselm, when Augustine says that even in the case of those who have identified God wrongly He is thought of in such a way that the thought attempts to reach something than which there is nothing better or loftier.[3] There is indeed a great similarity in the modes of expression employed by the two men, and there is good reason to believe that Anselm was influenced by his predecessor in this matter. But beyond the limited and largely verbal similarity it would be difficult to maintain that we have here a genuine source of the ontological argument, since whatever argument the passage contains is quite differently formulated. It is an argument regarding a being than which a better *is* not thought, not a being than which a better *cannot* be thought, and it is based on the universal consent to such a being rather than on the content of the conception itself,[4] which is the essence of Anselm's argument.

It is possible, however, to find a more substantial and less purely verbal source for the ontological argument in the works of Augustine, in a passage which has been too long neglected in this respect. The passage occurs in the seventh book of the *Confessions* where he is pursuing his search for the origin of evil, that is, of that which is liable to corruption. He says:

> For I was thus striving to discover the other things, as I had already discovered that the incorruptible is better than the corruptible, and so I confessed that You, whatever You are, are incorruptible. For no soul ever was able or will be able to think of anything that is better than You, who are the highest and best good. But since most truly and certainly the incorruptible is placed ahead of the corruptible, just as I had already placed it, I could now have reached in my thought something which was better than my God, if You were not incorruptible.[5]

In this passage, which seems to me the true Augustinian model for Anselm, there is a genuine argument involved, in this case for the incorruptibility of God, an attribute which places Him for Augustine beyond the range of evil. The mode of argumentation is very similar to that of Anselm. God is the greatest conceivable being and must therefore be incorruptible, since, if He were not, then another being possessing this perfection could be conceived that would be greater than God. The argument is based this time on the conception of God as the greatest conceivable being, just as it is in Anselm, the difference being that for incorruptibility Anselm substitutes existence. This substitution, as we shall see, is relatively simple, granted a different philosopher and the exigencies of another age, even though it was the introduction of existence into the argument by Anselm that made it both famous and controversial.

Let us therefore look a little further into the argument of Augustine and also see whether he in turn has any precursors and, in particular, whether there is anything in the Greek philosophical tradition to which he may be indebted. After proving that God is incorruptible, he points out that the substance of God can be touched in no way by corruption; not by any will, since whatever God wills is good; not by any necessity, since God cannot be forced unwillingly towards anything, seeing that His will does not transcend His power; and not by any unforeseen chance, since nothing is unforeseen to God, who knows all things. Why, he concludes, should we offer many arguments to show that the substance which is God is not corruptible, since if it were it would not be God?[6]

2. The Divine Perfection in Greek Thought to Plotinus

Underlying the argument of Augustine for the incorruptibility of God, and Anselm's ontological argument for God's existence as well, is a basic principle to the effect that God must possess the highest perfections of which we can conceive, with the attached corollary that a being to which any such perfection is lacking cannot be God. Such a principle can be perceived in Greek philosophy from a very early period, and it can even be traced back to pre-philosophical speculation. While we can be sure that this speculation contained rational elements, it is not possible—or necessary for our purposes—to determine the precise nature or extent of these elements. (Such an endeavor would involve us, for example, in the vexed question of the relation between Greek philosophy and the mythology that preceded it, and in various questions that are treated by the students of comparative religion and by the anthropologists.) This principle can be seen operating throughout the history of Greek philosophy, more in some thinkers than in others, and with one or another aspect of the divine perfection emphasized according to the requirements of the period and the purpose of the individual philosopher.

At the beginning of Greek literature, in the non-philosophical atmosphere of Homer, we can already perceive an adumbration of this principle in certain passages referring to the gods of the Olympian dynasty. In one place (*Odyssey* 5. 212–213) we read that it is not right (ἔοικεν) for mortal women to rival immortal goddesses in form and beauty. In a divine realm that is conceived in a highly anthropomorphic way it is not surprising that physical beauty should be prominent among the perfections attributed to the gods. But other prerogatives were also jealously guarded by the immortals. One recalls the flaying suffered by Marsyas at the hands of Apollo, a frequent subject in ancient literature and art, the tragic outcome of the mortal's challenge to the musical ability of the god who was proud to be the leader of the Muses. And Niobe, turned to stone, mourns forever the death of her children, which she brought about by boasting that her brood surpassed that of Leto, who was the mother of Artemis and Apollo.

This fundamental attitude continued into the period of philosophical speculation, but under the influence of the new approaches to reality and the new conclusions resulting therefrom the notion of God or the divine received a new content, and different perfections came to be included in it. Heraclitus offers a significant recognition of the new point of view in the fragment in which he states that the wise is unwilling and at the same time willing to be called by the name of Zeus.[7] That is to say, the first principle of all things which he has arrived at by a rational examination of the universe, and in particular the phenomenon of change, a principle which he identifies with his primal fire as well as the wise or God (though the equivalence is not quite certain), may be looked at in two ways: It has been lifted above and purified of the limitations and imperfections associated with the mythological conception of Zeus; but at the same time it has taken over, in the new scheme of things, the position of pre-eminence and authority traditionally occupied by the chief of the gods.

If Heraclitus, on the basis of available evidence, is more conscious of the contributions made by the new science of philosophy to the study of God than his philosophical predecessors had been, it is Xenophanes who expresses the principle we have been discussing in such a way that his stamp is henceforth never absent from the philosophy of God. Along with a series of statements about God that are clearly intended to be at variance with the older anthropomorphic view, he goes on to say (frag. 26) that it is not fitting that God should bustle about now hither now thither. He has arrived at a new conception of the power of God, which is exercised by immobility, not by the many motions in which the gods are engaged, let us say, in the *Iliad,* where they are represented as going from Mount Olympus to Troy and entering the battle array to assist their favorites. In fact, among the various perfections assigned by Xenophanes to God it is the divine immobility that expresses most significantly for him the advances made by the new way of thinking over the anthropomorphic view of the poets. This significance is not lost on his contemporaries even in non-philosophical literature, as in the tragedies of Aeschylus, where a strong trend to a less anthropomorphic portrayal of divinity is evident.[8] In his *Suppliants* (91–103) we see Zeus enthroned in majestic immobility, ruling the universe, as Xenophanes had put it (frag. 25), by the power of thought alone. In the spirit of Xenophanes (though not based on any

existing fragment) is the saying of the tragic poet
Euripides that God, if He is truly God, is in need
of nothing.[9]

When we look at Parmenides we do not find him
referring the term "God" or "divine" to being, which
is his special discovery in the history of western
thought. But, in fact, his formulation of the problem
of thought and being affected all subsequent speculation about God. And he does attribute to his "being"
the highest perfections of which he could think,[10] but
none more striking or more original than that "it is."
The immobility stressed in Xenophanes' conception
of God is carried over, but it is given a more solid
foundation in the very nature of "that which is" as
conceived by an intellect operating entirely within its
own realm. Parmenides' contribution to the perfection of being is nowhere better expressed than in his
statement (frag. 3) that it is the same thing that is
thought and that is. Whatever may be the precise
meaning of this controversial sentence, it indicates such
a relation between thought and its object that whatever is conceived as perfection in the order of intellect
must be referred to that of being. This point is amplified and confirmed a little later, when he states (frag.
6. 1) that that which can be spoken and thought must
necessarily be. He is here striking a keynote that
comes to characterize a whole tradition of philosophical thinking through the ages down to the present day.
This is the tradition commonly called Platonic, and,
however inexact such a term may be in its many uses,
it does have a certain relevance and value for us here.

As a result of his examination of human speech and

thought Plato posited the forms or ideas, those supra-sensible models in imitating which, and only in this way, the sensible world around us can make some claim to a kind of being. At the same time, since these forms, and not their sensible counterparts, are fixed and stable, they provide us with the only object of true knowledge that the intellect can have; and there can be said to be knowledge of the sensible world only insofar as amid its change and flux it manifests patterns of activity in which with the aid of the senses we can discern the imitation of the eternal forms. Plato has taken the principle first clearly enunciated by Parmenides and he has given it a much wider and more flexible application. He does not call the ideas by the name of God, and in this strict sense they do not belong to his theology. Nevertheless he has thereby made a most important contribution to later theology and to all philosophizing about God. There are many explicit statements in Plato, however, about God, and it would be well to mention some of them very briefly, since they continue the notion of the fitting stressed by Xenophanes, though sometimes only implicitly. In his discourse in the dialogue *Timaeus* on the origin of the universe he makes frequent reference to the craftsman responsible for the ordering of the universe, whom he calls God. In this highly metaphorical account it is essential to his purpose that the workings of nature be understood in terms of the goodness which underlies them and is indeed the very reason for them. With this in mind he affirms that the cause of the universe is good and, being without envy, desires that everything should be as good as possible.

We must think that the universe is beautiful and its maker good, for to think otherwise would be impious, he says, employing a word ($\theta\acute{\epsilon}\mu\iota\varsigma$) from the religious vocabulary to express an equivalent to Xenophanes' conception of that which is fitting to God.[11] In speaking of the education of the young in the *Republic* he repeats Xenophanes' criticisms of the poets, but with an emphasis on the goodness of God, insisting, in fact, that God and everything that belongs to God must be in every way the best (381B). In the *Laws* he again emphasizes the perfect goodness of God, or of the gods (900D), and he brands as impious the view that the material elements rather than God should be the first of all things (891C–D).

In philosophers such as Heraclitus, Xenophanes, and above all Plato the notion of what is fitting to God has been raised to an entirely new level of discourse. It is no longer in the realm of feeling, whether religious or esthetic, that we have seen in Homer and that indeed may be found throughout Greek literary history in the works of critics who are interested in what is fitting from the standpoint of form and style. New developments in philosophy and science have made it imperative that the chief cause of things, towards which the reason of man is tending, be considered in a way that is uniquely proper to it. From the point of view that will emerge in the centuries after Plato the Parmenidean and Platonic philosophies of being become most important, even though Parmenides has not applied the term "God" to his discovery, "that which is," and Plato, in his employment of basic terms like "God," "being," and "idea," has not seen fit to equate "God" with the others, for reasons that are related to the purpose served by these terms in his dialectic, but which we cannot go into here. But later philosophers, even those who called themselves Platonists, had no hesitation in making combinations and in obliterating distinctions quite at variance with the Platonic method as it may be observed in the works of the master himself. Even before the period of Neo-Platonism there is evidence that the Platonic ideas, the archetypes of sensible becoming, are moving closer to the God who was for Plato primarily a dynamic and moving force. No doubt under the influence of the Aristotelian God, who is a self-thinking thought, the ideas are placed within the mind of God, and it is then a natural step to identify them with God or at least with one facet of divinity, as is the case with Plotinus.

3. The Divine Perfection in Gregory of Nyssa

Unlike Plotinus, however, for whom a divine principle of unity and goodness was placed above and beyond a divine principle of thought and being, a Christian philosopher was not likely to place the being of God on a second level, since his philosophical convictions were formed with the scriptural passage in mind in which God defines Himself for human understanding: "I am who am" (Exodus 3. 14).[12] A good example of Christian speculation in this matter is Gregory of Nyssa—whose name I shall have occasion to use a number of times today—from the Cappadocian district of Asia Minor, a man who was thoroughly versed in all aspects of Greek culture, philosophical and otherwise. His work is especially pertinent to us here, since he adapts in a striking way many themes that were developed in earlier Greek thought to his explication of Christian doctrine; and, moreover, he brings us close to the time of Augustine himself, since he died just a few years before Augustine wrote the *Confessions*. Gregory, much as he is indebted to the thought of Plotinus in many matters, is unequivocal in affirming being of God, saying, for example, that "to be truly" is a proper identifying mark of divinity; [13] and, lest one be tempted in the manner of Plotinus to separate being and goodness, he states that being in the proper sense is the nature of the good.[14] He often quotes the statement, "I am who am," saying, for instance, that it offers one mark of true divinity; only that is truly divine, therefore, which is eternal and infinite in its being.[15]

This philosophy of being has its roots in the thought of Parmenides and of Plato, for both of whom likewise change and the time that goes along with change must be eliminated from a consideration of true being. For Parmenides says (frag. 8. 5) that being was not in the past and it will not be in the future, since it is now all at once; and Plato tells us (*Timaeus* 37E–38A) that men apply the terms "was" and "will be" wrongly to eternal being, whereas "is" alone is the correct term. But Gregory joins closely with his philosophy of the divine being the notion of what is fitting to God. Parmenides does not emphasize the conception of the fitting, and Plato's use of it is concerned primarily with God as the moving power in his dialectical ordering of the universe, and not with being, which, in the most usual sense of the term, is applied to the intelligible ideas in opposition to the sensible universe. Since the time of Plato the category of the "fitting" came to be used more and more with respect to God, so much so that a special term, for all practical purposes new, might now be employed, the θεοπρεπές, that is, the God-befitting. This adjective is used with great frequency in Gregory to qualify some word like "thought" or "conception" that has the being of God as its object, or the word "name" as it is applied to God's being. The significance of the "God-befitting" is indeed so powerful that for Gregory it can be quite sufficient to say that a certain conception or name is not God-befitting in order to dismiss it from further consideration.[16] We are moving in a realm of discourse reminiscent of the Parmenidean principle that what is thought and said must be, though in Gregory, of course, the rules that govern our thinking and saying are far more complex than they were in Parmenides, especially since we now have to take into account the intervention of Scripture with all that it reveals about the being of God. We have, in effect, in Gregory a fusion of Xenophanes and Parmenides, since for him only that which can properly be thought of God is actually thought of Him; anything else would be a contradiction that is not thought at all but only seems to be so. And we are not lacking echoes of the Platonic notion of "right" (*themis*) in this connection, as when we read that it is not right to attribute sense organs to God[17] or to deny that the divine nature is always good.[18] Moreover, instead of that which is

13

fitting or right or the opposite Gregory may speak of the "pious" ($\epsilon\vec{v}\sigma\epsilon\beta\acute{\epsilon}s$) or the "impious," employing extensively this related category applicable to thinking or speaking of God.

With this background in mind, and without forgetting the role played in Gregory's discussions of God by the proper mode of thinking and speaking about Him, let us look at a few types of expression he employs regarding God's being. First of all, with respect to the conception we have of Him, we must conceive Him as perfect in His goodness.[19] Whatever has the signification of the better must be included in our thinking about Him,[20] and whenever the inferior is predicated we no longer have a conception of God.[21] In the second place, we must likewise recognize that the name "God" signifies all perfection.[22] But, thirdly, we must grant that the complete perfection comprehended in our conception of God and expressed in the name "God" belongs to Him truly and not just in name.[23] In particular, we must admit that there is nothing greater than the divine nature to which it could change, because whatever is greater is in God.[24] Looked at negatively, we can say that God had no beginning, for otherwise He would not be God;[25] and if the divine nature were in any way changeable, it would not be divine.[26] In fact, he says, in the manner of Plotinus, it is characteristic of the divine nature alone to be diffusive of good, while it is itself in need of nothing else.[27]

In Gregory of Nyssa we see the culmination of a number of philosophical arguments, all of them adapted to the needs of a new time and, in particular, to the requirements of the situation, both philosophical and theological, in which Gregory found himself, since the doctrines stated above are directed against one or another heresy of his day. At the very center of his thought is the Parmenidean principle that what we can think and say is also that which exists. By means of this principle Parmenides arrived for the first time at changeless, eternal being; Plato set up the ideas as the archetypes of the whole world of becoming and the only true object of our knowledge; Plotinus devised a trinity of principles arranged in a hierarchy, the first of which, as the source of all being, must be beyond all being and therefore beyond the reach of thought as well. To a philosopher who does not belong to this tradition, in particular to an Aristotelian, such a procedure would appear as the confusing of two different orders, the logical and the metaphysical. Or, as Thomas Aquinas puts it in criticizing the ontological argument of Anselm, this is an unwarranted passing from the mind to reality.[28] To a philosopher, however, in the so-called Platonic tradition, amid all the differences that distinguish its members from one another, our conceptions and the words in which these conceptions are embodied enjoy a closer and more intimate relationship with their extra-mental counterparts than another type of philosopher would be prepared to admit. The modes in which our conceptions exist determine the modes of extra-mental reality. This is even true of Plotinus, for whom the first principle is utterly beyond all thought, and for Gregory of Nyssa, who never tires of cautioning us that human thought cannot hope to reach the essence of God.[29]

15

4. The Divine Perfection in Augustine

Augustine is the inheritor of the wealth accumulated in this tradition in the course of many centuries, and this is abundantly clear even when we cannot precisely determine whether or not he has read a given text, let us say, of Gregory of Nyssa, to whom he shows many resemblances, and not just in his philosophizing about God. Similarities may be found even to Xenophanes (frag. 11. 3), as when Augustine, following Varro, criticizes the anthropomorphic gods of the pagans for their thievings and adulteries in words that echo those of his long past predecessor.[30] More positively, he is often searching for the proper way of speaking of God, but finds that of all the things that are said of Him nothing can be said that is worthy of Him. We seek for a name that is fitting (*congruum*), but we do not find it.[31] We should note, however, the characteristic way in which Augustine is able to turn this point to his own advantage, in exclaiming that, despite the insuperable difficulty of saying anything about God, woe betide those who are silent about Him, since even the talkative are mute.[32] Plato and Gregory, when they discuss the first principle of all things, emphasize its overflowing goodness by stating that it is untouched by envy. Augustine does the same, associating envy on many occasions with the devil;[33] but at the same time as he removes from God every defect such as this he may counterbalance the negation by attributing to God, through a restrained and calculated anthropomorphism, some positive aspect of the defect, saying, for example, that God is jealous and

16

yet without concern.[34] Words of a basically religious character, which we have seen Plato employ to express what is proper or improper with regard to God, and which are used by Gregory in great profusion, are frequently found in Augustine, as when he says, speaking of free will, that it is unlawful (*nefas*) to believe that God has given man something He should not have given him,[35] or when he states that it is blasphemous (*sacrilegum*) to think that the archetypes of things are outside of God.[36]

It would, of course, be wrong to consider such passages non-philosophical merely because of the presence of words that have a religious background. In Gregory and Augustine (as in many of their predecessors), one need hardly repeat here, there is not to be found the sharp distinction between philosophy and theology elaborated at a later date. This same point is indicated by another passage, from his treatise on the Trinity, that is especially relevant to our purpose: Here Augustine is considering whether it is fitting (*dignum*) to call God substance. The name suggests to him a subject in which accidents have their existence, and therefore only changeable and non-simple things are called substances properly (*proprie*). If God is called substance properly (*proprie*), then He is not simple, and His attributes exist in Him as in a subject, greatness, omnipotence, goodness, and whatever else is attributed to God not improperly (*incongrue*). But, he counters, it is unlawful (*nefas*) to say that God is the subject for His goodness and that His goodness is not itself substance, or rather essence. It is clear then that God is called substance

17

improperly (*abusive*), and He should rather be called essence, which may be applied to Him truly and properly (*vere ac proprie*). So perhaps God alone should be called essence, for He alone truly is (*est*), because He is unchanging and because He revealed that name to Moses in saying, "I am who am."[37]

The main tenor of this passage, and of others like it, is philosophical, consisting in a rational examination of what is involved in being a substance or an essence, as Augustine understands these terms, or rather as he attempts to understand something of God and communicate this understanding by means of these terms. It is by now a well-established position, both in the Greek east and in the Latin west, that being or existence in the full sense of the word belongs to God alone,[38] and Augustine is in the forefront of those maintaining this position. His argumentation here hinges on such an attribution, and the scriptural reference to the name revealed to Moses is employed as confirmation. The word "unlawful" (*nefas*) is an echo of the Platonic theology, but this word and its equivalents have long since been taken over and their use greatly extended in the Christian tradition, as in Gregory of Nyssa. Most striking perhaps in this passage of Augustine is the frequency with which various words meaning "proper" or "improper" in some sense have been employed. Though we must think of Xenophanes, we might also be inclined to say that we are far removed from a thinker who tells us that it is not fitting for God to bustle about, now hither, now thither. Yet Augustine in general is very much preoccupied with setting God apart from moving things, and the frequency of his insistence on the divine immobility may even at times seem surprising. In this passage the term "substance" offers difficulty to him precisely because it suggests that God is numbered among things that are changeable as well as non-simple; and the reason offered for saying that God alone truly is, we should note, is that He is unchanging. But, though the frame of the "fitting" and the "proper" shows a distant kinship with Xenophanes, the actual content of Augustine's argument here is in a direct line from Parmenides and Plato, and likewise a number of other figures who elaborated the philosophy of being, such as Plotinus and Gregory. Any term applied to God is improper if it implies a diminution of His being, and a term is proper if it attributes true being to Him alone.

The interest in conceptions and terms that we have already noted in Gregory is found also in Augustine, in most cases even intensified because of his tendency to approach a problem in a psychological and introspective way. He tells us that during the period when he was struggling to come to a knowledge of God he came across Aristotle's work on the categories, which he tried to apply to an understanding of God without success.[39] He never tires of asking what is the meaning of the word "God." There is a word, he says on one occasion, that remains within the man himself as the sound is uttered by his lips, and this word has a spiritual power, that which the hearer understands from the sound rather than the sound itself. What is produced within your heart, he asks, when you hear the word "God"? You think of the very highest substance transcending all changeable creatures. And if I should ask you whether God is changeable or unchangeable you would answer without hesitation, "Perish the thought that I should believe or think God changeable; He is unchangeable." Your soul, however small, however attached perchance to things of the flesh, could answer only that God is unchangeable. How then were you able to flash forth to that which is above all changeable creatures so as to reply with certainty that God is unchangeable? What do you have within your heart when you think of a substance that is living, eternal, all-powerful, infinite, everywhere present and everywhere whole? When you think of those things this is the word "God" in your heart. While the word that consists of sounds passes away, that word which is signified by the sound remains.[40]

I may remark parenthetically that Augustine shares the preoccupation of later Neo-Platonism with the names that may properly be applied to God. Chiefly through the agency of the Pseudo-Dionysius the treatment of this problem finds its way even into the more Aristotelian precincts of Aquinas. As a result he too raises in this connection the question of propriety, one which has found a Platonic atmosphere the congenial one in which to thrive.[41]

5. Incorruptibility in Augustine and His Predecessors

It is significant that Augustine, with all the emphasis placed on the being of God in his works and in those of his predecessors, turns his attention to the incorruptibility of God, as we have seen, in the passage where he anticipates the ontological argument of Anselm. Part of the reason for this lies in his over-riding interest in the unchangeability that sets God apart from the world of created things, as we have noted in the passage just paraphrased, a preoccupation that is at least as pronounced as anything similar in Plato or Plotinus. But with the increasing interest in the role of man in the universe, in accordance with the Christian economy of salvation, as becomes very clear by the time of Gregory of Nyssa, terms like "mortality" and "corruptibility," both of them aspects of change, have a greater significance than before, since the death of man and his liability to sin come more and more into the main focus of attention. In particular, the Christian philosophers received from the pagan Neo-Platonists the doctrine that evil is not something positive but is rather a privation of being and goodness, and they soon adapted this to their own discussions of moral and metaphysical problems. Augustine, therefore, when he attempted to discover the origin of evil in human life, was by no means with-out predecessors in this matter, and the answers he gives show at every point their influence. It is not clear, however, how far their help was available to him in the early days of his search, and, in any case, the answers he was seeking were not merely theoretical, but practical ones that had to be worked into the pat-tern of his daily life.

Throughout the pages of the *Confessions* we can see this search going on constantly, but the account he offers at the beginning of the seventh book has a special interest for us here. He has given up the Manichaean doctrine that there is a supreme principle of evil as well as of good, and he no longer thinks of God as a body; but beyond this he does not know where to turn. He contrasts himself, the thinker, a man and the kind of man he was, with the object at which his thought was aiming, the most high, the one and true God. (We recall his statement that the soul, small as it is and burdened with the flesh, can know that God is unchangeable.) He then adds that, despite his perplexities, he believed in his innermost being that God is incorruptible, inviolable, and unchangeable. The reason for this was that, though he knew not whence or how this should be, he saw clearly and certainly that whatever can be corrupted is inferior to that which cannot; what cannot be violated he unhesitatingly placed ahead of that which can; and whatever suffers no change he considered better than that which can change. And while he was still obliged to think of God as extended somehow in space, though devoid of body, yet he thought of Him as incorruptible, inviolable, and unchangeable, which he placed ahead of their opposites.[42] As we look at the argumentation that Augustine offers here, namely, that God is incorruptible and so on because things that are so are better than those that are not, it is clear what the implied premise of his syllogism is: whatever is better must be attributed to God, a principle that is at least strongly implied in all the thinkers so far mentioned, and one that is stated quite explicitly by Gregory of Nyssa.

Since Augustine himself, as he tells us, did not know the source of these convictions he held so firmly, it is impossible for us to do more than speculate on this interesting and important question. It may be that certain doctrines of Plotinus were conveyed to him in the sermons of Ambrose, set forth no doubt in an appropriately Christian manner.[43] I have had suspicions from time to time that Augustine had some kind of contact with the works of Gregory of Nyssa, since in many ways the doctrines of Gregory seem to be natural predecessors to those of Augustine; but sufficient documentation is not available on this point to be convincing. In any case, whatever external influences may have affected Augustine at this crucial point in his spiritual life, we may be sure that the shape of his thoughts and beliefs was primarily the work of his own vigorous spirit, as we see it operating everywhere else. There is a question to what extent we may accept as historical the steps in his conversion as recounted in the *Confessions*. But this question does not concern us here. It is just as good for our purposes to know that at some time he held the convictions just stated, and that when he was writing the *Confessions* he considered these convictions to be a fitting prelude, historically or philosophically, to the formulation of the argument that we are undertaking to study.

He proceeds then to recall an argument against the Manichaean position that his friend Nebridius had used some time before while they were still in Carthage.[44] (The incident has an air of historicity, and it may have affected his way of thinking of the incorruptible, especially since he sees fit to report it at this point.) After describing the dilemma in which the Manichaeans had been placed by the argument of Nebridius, Augustine sums up his own reaction: If the Manichaeans should call God's substance incorruptible, then their whole position would be false and detestable (*exsecrabilia*); but if they should call it corruptible, that statement in itself would already be false and from the very start abominable (*abominandum*). Since this second alternative, Augustine indicates, would be the only way in which they could continue to maintain their basic teachings, they could not escape from the dilemma without committing a terrible sacrilege of heart and tongue. The unusually strong language he uses here, in applying the terms "abominable" and "terrible sacrilege" to the view that God's substance might be considered corruptible, shows how deep-seated and strongly felt was his conviction that the attribute of incorruptibility surely, one might almost say above all, must not be denied of God.

Though it is difficult to determine precisely whose teachings regarding God's incorruptibility were available to Augustine in his earlier life, we can perhaps be a little more sure why this question stirred his feelings so deeply. Along with his growing discontent with the Manichaeans, and his eventual revulsion towards them, he was constantly preoccupied with the problem of evil in his own life. He found himself perpetually falling short of an ideal that he saw quite clearly in his mind and that, sometimes at least, he desired ardently to attain. This discrepancy between the actual and the ideal in the moral order became for him the chief question to be answered in his pursuit of philosophical truth, and at the same time it provided him with his most important motivation. There are innumerable passages in the *Confessions* and other works to substantiate this; but most striking is the one that immediately follows his recalling the anti-Manichaean argument of Nebridius, where he tells graphically of his search for the cause of evil. He held firmly at the time in question that God, the true God, is incorruptible, unalterable, and in every way unchangeable. Though he had not yet arrived at the cause of evil, he knew that he could not seek it in such a way as to believe the unchangeable God changeable, lest he himself become the very thing he was trying to explain, namely, evil. This knowledge gave him the confidence and the certainty that the Manichaeans were wrong; for he had seen them, searching for the cause of evil, full of evil spite themselves, thinking that the substance of God suffered evil rather than that their own committed evil. He then outlines his first attempts to find the origin of evil in the free will, but tells how he was unable to reconcile this with the goodness of God. Despite his great discouragement, however, he was not cast down into the hell of error where no one confesses to God, thinking that God suffers evil rather than that man commits it.[45]

This somewhat detailed examination of the context preceding Augustine's actual argument for the incorruptibility of God has been necessary to show how it is to be understood, not only as a piece of theoretical reasoning, but also as an expression of the unhappiness and frustration he was experiencing in his whole life, moral as well as intellectual. With regard to the elements of the argument itself, we have noted how in one way or another they can be found in various

Greek philosophers, both pagan and Christian. As for the principle that whatever is best belongs to God, we can see this operating in a sense as far back as the earliest Greek literature; in particular, the notion of that which is fitting or proper to God, employed in an increasingly philosophical way by Xenophanes and Plato, reaches a climax in the "God-befitting" of Gregory of Nyssa. The acceptance of incorruptibility as such a perfection has its roots in the very origins of philosophy itself, namely, in the search for something that abides amid the coming to be and passing away of everything in the world around us. Terms like "unalterable" and "impassive" become standard predicates of the first principle early in Greek thought. This general tendency of philosophy is given a special direction by the dialectical use of the good as a first principle by Plato, especially in the *Timaeus* and the *Republic*,[46] and by the subsequent metaphysical use of the good in Plotinus. In Plotinus a moral force is also attached to the good, that which is farthest removed from change and corruption, in his explanation of evil, and this is taken over and considerably amplified by the Christian philosophers, who, like Gregory, must deal with the problem of sin and salvation, that is, with the moral significance of the corruptible and the incorruptible, such as we meet it in Augustine.

The three supplementary considerations offered by Augustine to confirm his proof for the incorruptibility of God likewise have distant origins in Greek speculation, both philosophical and pre-philosophical. (1) The statement that God can will only the good goes back at least as far as Plato;[47] and the very positive

26

doctrine of Plotinus on this point, despite a different understanding of what the freedom of the first principle means, is reflected in the Christian predecessors of Augustine.

(2) As for the notion that God cannot be forced against His will through a lack of power, this has had a varied history in Greek thought. As early as Homer there is a groping for a supreme being that surpasses all things in power. Zeus is represented as telling all the other gods and goddesses that their combined power would not avail against him (*Iliad* 8. 18–27); and he has only to nod his head to make Olympus quake (*Iliad* 1. 528–530). But Xenophanes found the motions by which the Homeric gods exercise their activities too anthropomorphic, and for him God remains without motion in the same place, without toil stirring all things by the power of His mind. The metaphorical craftsman called by the name of God in Plato's *Timaeus* is in some way faced by the force of Necessity, which is connected with the materials that must be employed in the fashioning of the universe;[48] but the metaphors involved in this conception, however they may be interpreted, do not militate against the far-reaching extent of the divine power. Aristotle, who sees in the Homeric description of the overwhelming power of Zeus an anticipation of his own unmoved mover,[49] says of this cause of his that it moves by being loved,[50] thereby carrying the effortless exercise of power propounded by Xenophanes into a completely philosophical conception of the highest cause of all things as the end towards which they are striving. Later developments of the notion of divine power, such as

are found in the Stoics, are widely reflected in poetry and other non-philosophical literature. In Plotinus, as one would expect, the power of the first principle is absolute.[51] This is true also for the Christian philosophers, though their view of the divine omnipotence is naturally affected by their conception of a very personal God; and even before Augustine they encounter problems, such as are doubtless in the mind of Plato, in reconciling God's omnipotence with the existence of evil.

(3) Finally, there is the question of God's knowledge, so that nothing can happen by any unforeseen chance. Anaxagoras was the first philosopher to make mind explicitly the moving cause of all things, controlling and arranging them through knowledge. Plato, having his craftsman fashion the sensible universe in imitation of eternal models, begins the tradition of exemplarism. Aristotle's God, the self-thinking thought, is not said to have any knowledge of the universe, but such knowledge is not to be ruled out. Before the time of Plotinus the Platonic ideas had been placed in a divine mind; that is where they are for Plotinus, though this mind, despite its perfection of being and of knowledge, takes second rank to the first cause, which transcends all being and knowledge. The Plotinian hierarchy of divine principles is unified in the God of the Christian thinkers; and they, like him, hold that there is a providence inasmuch as the divine intelligence, containing the archetypes of all things, knows and directs all things. Here also special problems arose in the Christian tradition because of the existence of evil in a universe watched over by the providence

28

of God. All in all, there was no paucity of materials available to Augustine in constructing his argument for the incorruptibility of God.

6. The Greek Background of the "Ontological" Argument

It is possible now to raise the question in what does the ontological argument and its predecessors consist, and then what is the position to be assigned to Augustine in the long-continued development of this argument. There is a basic principle present in every argument of this kind, namely, that the highest perfection or perfections are to be predicated of God, that is, the highest cause. This principle is employed as the major premise of the argument, and it is presented as self-evident, though some kind of explanation may be offered for it, with the notion of "fitting" and "proper" expressed or implied. The particular perfection to be predicated is set forth in the minor premise, which will vary with the thinker and the purpose for which he is constructing the argument. The major premise is therefore a kind of form, which comes down through the tradition I have been discussing, to be given from time to time a different content.

In the poems of Homer, where the conception of the gods is highly anthropomorphic, it is to be expected that physical beauty will be considered a prominent attribute of the divine nature. When we read that it is not fitting for a mortal woman to vie with immortal goddesses in beauty, we are being told that the highest beauty is fittingly attributed to goddesses. On the other hand, since Xenophanes is rebelling against this anthropomorphism, and especially against the excessive motion that seems to him to characterize the gods of the poets, he criticizes this motion as unfitting and offers in turn a conception of God as ruling the universe with majestic immobility through the power of thought alone.

But it is Parmenides who, dissatisfied with the compromises between being and becoming in which his predecessors seemed to become involved, arrives for the first time at a genuinely philosophical conception of the complete perfection of that which is. He is guided into the depths of this new realm of thought, not by ill fortune ($\mu o \hat{\iota} \rho a$), but by right ($\theta \acute{\epsilon} \mu \iota \varsigma$, a word echoed, as we have seen, by Plato and Gregory) and by justice ($\delta \acute{\iota} \kappa \eta$).[52] He is thus able to avoid the other path, that towards non-being, a path which cannot be explored, one that is unthinkable and nameless.[53] Although Anaxagoras may not have been the first to give mind some kind of role in the universe, it is he who gives it the actual domination over the workings of nature (despite the reservations of Plato and Aristotle on this point[54]). In order to fulfill the functions that he thought such a moving power must have he determined that it should be unmixed with the elements of the universe and entirely independent of them; only in this way can it control all things. For the same reason it must be considered the finest and purest of all things, and it has complete knowledge and the highest power.[55]

Plato, in his endeavor to understand the universe in

terms other than the partly or wholly mechanistic ones of most of his predecessors, sets it within a framework of reason and goodness, asking us, in the myth of the *Timaeus,* to view it as proceeding from the ordering hand of a divine craftsman, who it would be impious to think is other than good, and who holds back nothing within his power from his handiwork in a spirit of envy. This account is supplemented by that of the *Republic* in which the idea of the good is elevated to the highest position, placed even "on the other side of being."[56] The Platonic good is crystallized in the transcendent good of Plotinus, which is complete and self-sufficient, lacking nothing and communicating the overflow of its perfection to all things.[57] This principle is likewise the most perfect unity, even going beyond intelligence, in which we are able to distinguish the duality of knower and known. The cause for Plotinus must always be simpler than the effect, and so the first cause must be the simplest of all.[58] But it is not called one in the sense that unity is predicated of something other than itself, as happens in our experience of unity. No name, he says, is truly proper ($\pi\rho\sigma\hat{\eta}\kappa\sigma\nu$) to it; but, since we must call it by some name, we may properly ($\pi\rho\sigma\sigma\eta\kappa\acute{o}\nu\tau\omega\varsigma$) call it "one" with the necessary reservations.[59]

Of the philosophers who attribute one or another perfection to God for reasons they consider good and sufficient, none is more conscious of his motives for doing so and of the propriety or impropriety of a particular attribution than is Gregory of Nyssa. For this reason he may be taken as representing the stage immediately preceding Augustine in the development of the ontological argument, as indeed he precedes him shortly in time. He is constantly making explicit use, as we have seen, of the principle that whatever is better or greater is in God, or that whatever is better in our conception or in the meaning of a term must be considered as belonging to God. Most significant perhaps from our point of view is his interest in what is meant by the term "God," with the complementary statement that a perfection must belong to God truly, not just in name. (Is he here anticipating that aspect of Anselm's argument that seemed to Aquinas an illegitimate passing from the mind to reality?) He also offers examples of the corresponding negative position, namely, that if some perfection is lacking the being in question cannot be God.

7. The "Ontological" Argument in Augustine and Anselm

Augustine follows along in this tradition, taking over the formulations that had been made explicit in the stage that Gregory had reached, and focusing them on the perfection of God that was most relevant to him at a time when he was feeling most keenly his own corruptibility. The mode of expression likewise is more concentrated than the more diffuse statements of Gregory, since Augustine compresses both the positive and the negative positions of Gregory into the same argument. Gregory's statement (if we may make a composite one for him) that all perfections belong to God as both the greatest and the greatest conceivable being is reflected in the argument of Augustine as a whole regarding a single perfection of God. On the other hand, Gregory's statement (again composite) that if a perfection is lacking we are clearly not dealing with God is expressed by Augustine in saying that if God were not incorruptible then he could think of some other being that was better than God. But this negative position enters Augustine's argument in such a way that it occupies the chief place, and indeed through it, and only through it, is the other, more positive position expressed. That is to say, Augustine does not declare in so many words that God as the best conceivable being must be incorruptible; he says rather that if He were not incorruptible then we could think of another being better than He is, though we really know that God is indeed the best conceivable being. It is this absurdity into which we are led that constitutes the argument in Augustine. Though all the materials for the argument have been provided for him by the tradition of which he is a part, it is he who has devised its distinctive form.

It is this very form that is taken over by Anselm, but with a change of content, that is, with the substitution of God's existence for His incorruptibility. This is clear from a simple comparison of the two arguments. For Anselm God is that than which a greater (*maius*) cannot be thought; for Augustine, with the more vivid active voice, no soul can think of anything that is better (*melius*) than God. For Anselm, if one does not attribute actual existence to such a being, then one could think of an actually existing being that would be greater; for Augustine, if one does not attribute incorruptibility to such a being, then one could think of an incorruptible being that would be better. Above all, in both thinkers the essence of the argument consists in pointing out the absurdity that one falls into when the perfection in question is denied of the being that is held to be the best or the greatest that can be thought.

But, despite the similarity in form of the two arguments, some might wonder (though others would not be greatly concerned by this point) how direct the dependence of Anselm on the text of Augustine is,[60] thinking, for example, that Anselm uses the adjective "greater" (*maius*) and expressions that are passive and relatively impersonal, such as "that than which a greater cannot be thought"[61] and "in the intellect," whereas Augustine uses the adjective "better" (*melius*)[62] and more active and lively expressions, such as "no soul could ever think" and "I could have reached in my thought." Even though such variations would be in no way surprising, granted the natural differences in temperament and style of the two men, still we should read on a few lines further in the text of Anselm. Having proved that God exists, he proceeds to prove in similar fashion that He cannot be thought of as not existing. For if He could, then He would be less than a being whose non-existence would be impossible to think of. So we would fall once more into the contradiction of saying that some being was thought of as greater than the being than which a greater cannot be thought. Thus God exists so truly that His non-existence cannot be thought. And rightly so, says Anselm. For if some mind could think of something better than God, then the creature would rise above and pronounce judgment on the creator, which is completely absurd.[63] In this sentence Anselm shifts from "greater" (*maius*), which he has used constantly to this point, to the "better" (*melius*) of Augustine, and the construction, changing to the active voice, becomes very similar to one of Augustine, "some mind" taking the place of "any soul" as the subject. It is even possible that when Anselm speaks of the creature rising above the creator to sit in judgment on Him he is offering a more dramatic version of the corresponding statement Augustine makes, namely, that he could have reached something in his thought that was greater than God (if God were not incorruptible).[64] Finally, Anselm's characterization of the opposing position as contradictory (*convenire non potest*) and completely absurd (*valde absurdum*) makes explicit for the first time the *reductio ad absurdum* which is the foundation, not only of the two arguments Anselm has just used, but also of their prototype in Augustine.

It is interesting to note, from the historical point of view, that Anselm seems, and quite sincerely, to be unaware of any indebtedness on his part to Augustine for his ontological argument. He tells in his preface to the work of the deep meditations that preceded his discovery of this argument, or rather, the argument's forcing itself upon him.[65] This is in a way ironical, since he was certainly aware of his indebtedness in general to Augustine, and of another of his works he even says that there is nothing in it that is not in agreement with the writings of the Fathers and especially of Augustine.[66] We can well believe that, despite the similarity of the arguments of the two men, Anselm did not have the text of Augustine before him (and this indeed makes the similarity more striking). He was so well acquainted with the works of Augustine over a long period of time that Augustinian modes of argumentation and even choice of words had become second nature to him. The struggles he relates so graphically of the argument's attempts to come to the surface of his mind were, to a considerable extent, an effort on his part to bring to bear on the problem he faced all his resources, natural and acquired, and the latter were, directly or indirectly, strongly Augustinian. The form the argument took, when it finally came to birth, was the one that had been given to it by Augustine, though its antecedents are much older. Anselm gave this form a new content, that of God's existence. But the notion that only God truly is is also readily available in Augustine (as well as in Gregory and many others, who employed both philosophical and scriptural reasons to support this position; and it comes ultimately from Greek thinkers who knew nothing of the Scriptures.)

Thus both the form and the content of the ontological argument are in Augustine, one may say, though separately. Anselm had not the imperative need to prove the incorruptibility of God that inspired Augustine; he used the argument for what was most pressing to him, that is, to prove God's existence. Even the terminology that he required for his argument is, as we have seen, Augustinian. It may be clear, therefore, that pervading the argument of Anselm there is a philosophical spirit that relates it to Augustine and to a long tradition before him. In the entire process by which the ontological argument came finally to be formulated there are at least three well-defined stages. In the first of these, of which Gregory of Nyssa may be taken as representative, a number of notions about God that had been developed during the whole course of Greek philosophy are articulated and applied to the great problem of fusing the philosophical and scriptural heritages amid a heightened awareness of the propriety or impropriety of conceptions and of terms, especially as these have reference to God. So we find, in particular, two Gregorian and generally Greek principles carefully formulated and constantly employed, namely, that all perfection belongs to God, and whatever being is imperfect or inferior cannot be God. Next Augustine combines these two principles and fashions from them his argument for God's incorruptibility, based, as we noted, on a *reductio ad absurdum*. Finally Anselm takes the Augustinian form and gives it a new content, which is itself to be found in Augustine and in others as well.

As for the basic motivation underlying the whole tradition from which the ontological argument springs, it is easy enough, as we saw, to find a tendency even before the beginning of philosophy to ascribe to God or to some kind of divine principle one or more perfections that are considered outstanding. But it would be wrong to forget that with the advent of philosophy a pre-existing habit of mind was given a new depth and an entirely new significance through a critical examination of human knowledge and its object. This strictly philosophical outlook can be noted by the time of Parmenides, who strikes the keynote for an entire tradition of philosophical and theological thinking when he declares that what can be spoken and thought must be. Such a view takes over the pre- or the non-philosophical category of the "God-befitting," which seems in Xenophanes also to have achieved some philosophical significance, and applies it in the strictest sense to that which truly is. Thus Parmenides' description of that which is and of the attributes that belong to it could never be forgotten from that point forward by philosophers of the western world when they spoke of God, and in particular not by those who belonged to the tradition which we have been discussing. The use made of his principle by Parmenides himself shows that the mind is not intended by him to establish arbitrary correspondences between itself and reality. But he and the tradition of which he is a part insist that when the mind is operating at the highest level of its activity, that is, on the highest objects of its knowledge, then there is a correspondence between thought and reality. Thus we have the preoccupation with true, that is, suprasensible being as the proper object of the intellect in a certain group of philosophers, and the eventual result of this preoccupation is the argument of Anselm. It is not accidental that Augustine, in the course of his argumentation, declares that *no soul* ever was able or will be able to think of anything which is better than God, and, a little later, that he himself would have been able to reach *in thought* something which was better than God if God were not incorruptible. This is the same interest in the conception we have of God already noted in Gregory of Nyssa, and it is clearly reflected in the terminology of Anselm.

8. The Moral Universe of Augustine

We may then wonder why Augustine, with philosophies of "true being" before and after him, and with such a philosophy of being to be found in his own works, should have devised the forerunner of Anselm's argument for the special purpose of proving God's incorruptibility. The reason is not at all that he neglects the being of God; he maintains unequivocally, as we have seen, that only God truly is. The explanation lies partly in the tradition that Augustine was following, partly in his handling of that tradition. In that tradition as a whole the principal set of opposites in all spheres is that of being and becoming. This has its beginning in Parmenides, but it receives its chief impetus from the philosophy of Plato. Then the opposites of being and becoming collect around themselves still other sets of opposites, one and many, unchangeable and changeable, and so on. Nowhere is this more evident than in the dialectic of Plotinus, in which one or another set of contraries is constantly being applied to a higher and a lower level of perfection within his hierarchy. These contraries are very often employed by him to differentiate various forms of life, a term which is used on all levels as synonymous with perfection. This flexible use of "life" is found also in Gregory of Nyssa and in others, and it gives their employment of contraries a whole new set of associations that are not found in philosophers who speak merely of various levels of being. At the same time in the Christian philosophers this attention to "life" is focused more and more on man and the moral problems he faces during his sojourn on earth. This anthropocentrism affects the use of the traditional contraries in such a way that the opposition is frequently limited to God and man as the two levels of life which are most relevant; and the Platonic statement from the *Theaetetus* (176B) that man should try to become like God by becoming just and holy and wise is constantly reaffirmed and reinterpreted within a Christian context.[67]

The contrast between human corruptibility and the divine incorruptibility is, therefore, by no means new in Augustine. He applies it, however, to himself in a concrete and personal way that had never been seen before. This is especially true of the *Confessions,* which shows everywhere a tendency to self-analysis and introspection, since it recounts Augustine's inner pilgrimage and above all his struggles, both practical and speculative, with the problem of evil. Within this context, though the physical universe is by no means excluded, it is Augustine himself who is placed at the center of the realm of becoming, and that which chiefly characterizes this realm for him is, not the more objective change and flux of a Heraclitus, and not even the moral changes that constitute the general problem of human salvation for a Gregory, but the changes in his own life that lead to his own sin and moral corruption. However much he has noted this corruption in the Manichaeans and others, these personal changes of his *are* becoming for Augustine. Since his own corruptibility is equated with becoming, it is natural that the divine incorruptibility should be equated with being. Have we not here a moral counterpart to the *Timaeus* of Plato? Instead of the cosmic opposition of being and becoming we are given the opposition, equally cosmic but in a moral universe, of the incorruptible and the corruptible. Instead of an imitation of being by the world of becoming that depends entirely on the activity of a divine craftsman we are given an imitation, or a hoped-for imitation, of the incorruptible by the corruptible that depends in large measure—and this is the chief difference—on the free choice and cooperation of the corruptible itself. Just as Plato employs the phenomena of the physical world to create a dialectical universe in which reason bends the blind forces of necessity to its own purposes, so Augustine applies his dialectic to the events of his personal life to create a moral universe in which he, under the providence of God, brings the blind forces within his own nature under the control of reason. Within this universe, just as his own corruptibility *is* becoming, so incorruptibility *is* being. It is the standard by which his actions are seen to be wanting and the ideal towards which he is or should be striving. But the incorruptible, he also perceived in some way, is the cause of the corruptible, and this offered a special problem of its own. Some philosophers have found an "ontological scandal," as it has been called, in the very existence of becoming in the face of being. So Augustine, like many another, found a moral scandal in the existence of the corruptible when he knew that incorruptibility exists.

But if incorruptibility *is* being in the moral universe of Augustine, it is also God. As we may say of certain types of person that for them money or honor or something similar is their God, so for Augustine, within his moral universe, incorruptibility is God, and not just in a rhetorical sense, however fond we know he was of rhetoric. Lest this seem a strange expression, we should recall that for Augustine there are no accidents in God, but everything is substance or essence. Incorruptibility—though it be negative as we think it—is therefore substantial, just as are goodness, intelligence, and so on, and we must not think, as Augustine often warns us, that God is a subject in whom various accidents have their existence. However much some might be inclined to think, as Aquinas does, that being is the name applied most appropriately to God,[68] this would be to overlook the dialectical scheme Augustine has fashioned in the *Confessions,* based as this is, not on any abstract consideration of the nature of God, but on the conviction of a man torn apart by years of struggle and amidst it all attempting to understand himself and the meaning of that struggle. Within the very vivid and concrete consciousness that he had from day to day and year to year of his own corruptibility the conviction that incorruptibility exists was a source of perplexity and frustration; but without this conviction he would have been without hope. Therefore, though he uses the conventional style of predication in saying that God is incorruptible, the sense of his argumentation may be expressed by saying that for him incorruptibility exists and it is given the name of God. A kind of analogy to this may be found in other philosophers who argue to God's existence, as in the five ways Thomas Aquinas employs to prove God's existence. He proves that there is a prime mover and adds that all men understand this to be God; and to the proofs that there is a first efficient cause, and so on, he makes similar additions.[69] So for Augustine, though his method of proof is, of course, not the *a posteriori* one of Aquinas, the existence of incorruptibility is proved within the moral universe of search and suffering, and this is called by the name of God.

9. The "Ontological" Character of Augustine's Argument

If there is any truth in this, I should like to go one step further. I have already suggested that Anselm was in some sense dependent on Augustine—though unconsciously so—for both the form and the content of his ontological argument, as well as for its terminology, but that he found the form and the content separately in the works of his master. Certainly it was Anselm's introduction of existence into the framework of the argument that gave rise to the name later applied to it and likewise to the controversies attending it. (Though Anselm's argument was attacked immediately by the monk Gaunilo, there is no record that Augustine's argument was ever so treated.) But if the argument proposed by Augustine did not prove to his satisfaction the existence of an incorruptible substance called God, of what value was it to him? And if it proved God's existence from our conception of Him as the best possible being, is there any reason, apart from one of convention, why we should withhold the name "ontological" from it? (It goes without saying that the name we give the argument has nothing to do with our accepting or rejecting it, since even the opponents of Anselm's argument may call it "ontological.") We should not think, for example, that Augustine is merely declaring that a God whose existence he has already proved is to be given the attribute of incorruptibility. There is no indication that this argument is dependent on any other, and indeed such a view would be imposing on Augustine something like the Thomistic method, whereby a perfection like incorruptibility is attributed to God only after His existence has been proved. The existence of incorruptibility, which, since it is taken in a substantial sense, is identical with God, is the goal of this single argument, and it is not intended to depend on any other, just as Anselm in his preface indicates is true of his argument.[70] The use of the term "incorruptibility" instead of "being" or "existence" should not rule out the name "ontological," since incorruptibility *is* the existence that Augustine arrives at by reasoning within his moral universe out of the depths of the human situation in which he is immersed. In these days one would even be tempted to add that an argument having such an origin as this is more deserving of the name "ontological," if this may mean "existential," than one that is so abstract as that of Anselm, lacking as it does the clear-cut marks of the human condition that characterize the argument of Augustine.[71]

One might even venture to suggest that, while it is

easy to think that Anselm's argument, because of its explicitness and abstractness, is a more fully developed and therefore a more perfect version of Augustine's, we may also look on it in another way. By its very abstractness has it not also lost some of the power that is found in the more concrete argument of Augustine? Even without Anselm's own description of how his argument originated we can think of Augustine's argument as lying in a half active, half dormant state within Anselm's spirit for a long time. But when it finally emerges into the light of day it has left behind the elements that make Augustine's argument really "existential," because it has been filtered through a mind that is relatively untouched— as far as our evidence goes—by temptation and moral upheaval.

Since the two arguments, as is clear from the entire tradition to which they belong, cannot be understood in isolation from the whole manner and spirit of philosophizing that produced them, Gaunilo's piece-meal objection to the argument of Anselm must be considered largely irrelevant. To grant existence, for example, to an island surpassing all existing lands in perfection is not the same thing at all for Anselm or Augustine or Parmenides as granting it to the greatest conceivable being, which is the highest object of human thought.[72] The objection of Gaunilo illustrates the temptation and the danger of selecting an individual philosophical doctrine for criticism. Such a criticism may call attention to unanswered questions and unresolved problems in a given philosophical approach, or especially to the fact that its view of reality is necessarily a partial one. But it overlooks the integral nature of a well-constructed philosophy and the likelihood that any individual doctrine will stand or fall with the whole approach to which it belongs. Gilson, in one of his many perceptive discussions of Augustine's method, remarks that it opens the way for Anselm's metaphysical speculations, which seek to discover the existence of God in the very idea we have of Him. He adds—possibly not having in mind the passage from the *Confessions*—that, while Augustine does not develop the proof of Anselm himself, he is certainly proceeding in a direction that in the normal course of events leads to that proof.[73] As Gilson suggests, there was a certain inevitability that after an Augustine an Anselm or Anselms would sometime come along. And it was just as inevitable that there would be others to oppose them. For every Anselm, like Bonaventure and Descartes, who steps on the stage, there is a Gaunilo, like Aquinas or Kant, lurking in the wings, and there is no reason to believe that this will not always be so.

We should understand that it is not our task here to inquire into all the subtleties of Anselm's argumentation, but to see only how it could have developed out of that which Augustine employs in the *Confessions,* and how indeed the argument of Augustine may in a very genuine sense be called ontological. Gilson has said that the argument of the *Proslogion* cannot properly be understood except in the epistemological atmosphere of Anselm's treatise *On truth.*[74] Whether everyone would agree with him in this or not, we can surely say that an examination of the atmosphere which surrounds a philosophical work may give us highly relevant information about the precise meanings and associations of the terms the philosopher employs and about his characteristic method of philosophizing. But in our study of philosophical atmosphere is it not also profitable to go beyond the works of the philosopher himself and examine his position in relation to his predecessors and even his successors? Proceeding in this spirit we have seen, I think, how the argument for God's existence that we call ontological not only follows in a direct line from an argument of Augustine, but indeed may in a very real sense be considered his discovery.

II. The Flight of the Soul

1. The Divine Origin of the Soul in Greek Thought to Plotinus

When Augustine states, in propounding his version of the ontological argument, that no *soul* (*anima*) has the power to think of something which is better than God, we might suppose that "soul" is used here as equivalent either to "mind," which indeed recurs in the argument of Anselm, or even to "person," especially since he says a few lines later that *he* could have reached in his thought something that was better than God, if God were not incorruptible. Yet in so doing we would be overlooking the associations attached to "soul" in Augustine himself and in a long-standing tradition. There exists, in fact, a close parallel in the development of the notions of God and of soul in western thought. We are told by a sceptic of the second century after Christ, Sextus Empiricus, that Aristotle traced men's thought about the gods back to two sources, phenomena of the soul (ψυχή) and of the heavens; for, regarding the soul, when it is separated from the body in sleep or at the moment of death it assumes its true nature and foresees the future, as we see in Homer. For these reasons men came to suspect that something divine existed, something that was like (ἐοικός) the soul and of all things the most knowing.[75]

Though we may wonder how much of Aristotle's actual language survives in the paraphrase of Sextus, the fact is that a certain kinship of the human soul to God or to the divine is evident at an early point in Greek speculation. Quite different from the Homeric soul, which on the death of the man goes off to a shadowy existence in the underworld, is the soul believed in by the adherents of the so-called Orphic mystery-religion—the assignment of the name "Orphic" is often uncertain—as early as the sixth century before Christ. Though the evidence for this religion is of a later date —some of it much later—and not entirely consistent, it indicates with some probability that the soul for the Orphics is godlike in its essential nature, but that it was obliged to leave its divine abode because of some transgression and descend to earth, where it inhabits a succession of bodies, human and otherwise, until by its suffering in the "wheel of birth" it has expiated its primeval sin. The Orphic religion offered the initiate a means of escaping from the "wheel of birth" through its rites of purification, so that his soul could return more directly to its rightful home.[76] A fragment from the fifth-century lyric poet Pindar offers the earliest statement of this new view of the nature of the soul. He says that, while the body of every man is subject to overpowering death, a living image (εἴδωλον) of life survives, since it alone comes from the gods. It sleeps while the limbs are active, but to those who are asleep it reveals in many a dream the joys and sorrows that are to come.[77] Many beliefs and practices similar to those of the Orphics were adopted by the Pythagoreans of southern Italy and joined with their philosophical and scientific studies to form a special "way of life," in which great stress was laid on the purification of the soul. Empedocles likewise, alongside his poem *On nature*, has set forth in the *Purifications*, also in poetic form, how the "spirit" or "demigod" (δαίμων) has defiled itself and been banished from the seats of the blessed to wander for thrice ten thousand years and be born in the course of time in all kinds of shapes of mortal things. "Of their number," he says, "I too am now one, an exile from the gods and a wanderer."[78]

But it is Plato who utilizes this kind of religious tradition in such a way that it makes its greatest contribution to philosophy. In many places, for example in the myth of the *Phaedrus,* he presents a similar view of the soul's nature, its origin and its destiny, but always carefully adapted to serve his own purposes. Man cannot be looked on in the mechanistic way of the atomists, but must be thought to possess within himself a principle of human personality which is more truly himself than the body is. This principle, for which he takes over the name of "soul," being influenced doubtless in so doing by the usefulness he found in the religious conception of the soul, makes man a moral agent responsible in some measure for his own fate, and it must be given the most careful attention by him throughout his life. The type of purification of the soul that Plato himself has in mind may be illustrated by the passage from the *Theaetetus* (176A–B) already referred to: Since evils cannot exist among the gods, but hover always around mortal nature and this earth, we should try to flee from here to there as quickly as possible; this flight consists in becoming like God as far as we can, and to become like Him is to become just and holy and wise. This kind of moral exhortation underlies the Platonic use of the Orphic or another religious psychology and eschatology, which there is no reason for taking literally, whether expressed by Plato in an obvious myth or otherwise. If one takes it literally, in whole or in part, then it is easy to construct "the religion of Plato," though this is likely to be at the expense of Plato's philosophy and his sense of philosophical method. The words placed by Plato in Socrates' mouth in these matters may even be sceptical: The doctrine of the mysteries that men are in a kind of prison and must not try to escape is not easy for him to understand (*Phaedo* 62B); to maintain that the stories of the after-life are just as he has recounted them would not be fitting for a man of good sense (*Phaedo* 114D).[79] But one can still say that the philosopher practices for death all his life (*Phaedo* 64A), and by the philosophical import of this Plato indicates that, like the

Pythagoreans, he has in his own way made philosophy a "way of life."[80]

Whatever we may think, however, of the employment of the Orphic or other mythology by Plato, the important point for us is that in later Platonism the so-called religious element in Plato is very important, though it may be used more literally than was true for Plato, and, in any case, it may serve to elucidate and communicate philosophical doctrines that are different from his. As an example of this we may look at a passage from Plotinus' treatise *On the beautiful* (1. 6), a work that has had a very wide influence in subsequent philosophy and literature down to our own time. The discussion of beauty leads—quite naturally for Plotinus—to the question of the beauty of the soul, and this, he tells us, consists in the soul's emancipation from the passions (1. 6. 5). There is an ancient teaching that every virtue, including even wisdom, is a form of purification, he says, and he goes on to show how several virtues may be explained as different ways in which the soul is lifted above bodily concerns. In short, one may say that as the soul becomes good and beautiful it becomes like God (1. 6. 6). We should make the greatest effort, therefore, lest we be deprived of the vision of the beautiful, for which one should be ready to renounce all earthly power and glory (1. 6. 7). Coming now to the crucial point of his discourse, he asks in what manner ($\tau\rho\acute{o}\pi o\varsigma$) or by what device ($\mu\eta\chi\alpha\nu\acute{\eta}$) one may achieve the vision of this inaccessible ($\dot{\alpha}\mu\acute{\eta}\chi\alpha\nu o\nu$) beauty, which remains within its sacred precincts and does not come out for all, even the profane, to gaze upon. (This is one of the many allusions Plotinus makes in this treatise to the mysteries.) Let him who is able search for it within, leaving outside the vision of his bodily eyes. Let our flight be to our beloved fatherland, he exclaims, employing an expression from Homer, a flight like that made by Odysseus from the enchantress Circe or from Calypso, despite all their blandishments. Our fatherland is there whence we have come, and our father too is there. But what form of travel can our flight take? We cannot rely on our feet, which take us from one place to another; nor is there any need to make ready a carriage drawn by horses or a sailing vessel. We must dispense with all these and close our eyes, waking in ourselves another kind of see-ing (ὄψιν), which all men possess but few men employ (1. 6. 8). [81] We must withdraw into ourselves and see where we are lacking in beauty within, and then rid ourselves of every imperfection. When we have done this and become pure vision itself, then, with no further need for a guide, we gaze intently and see. For this is the only eye that looks upon the real beauty (1. 6. 9).

2. The Flight of the Soul in Augustine

In 1934 Father Henry, who initiated this series of lectures five years ago,[82] pointed out in a pioneering work, which is still of great value, that Augustine in a number of places follows closely some of the ideas and even terminology used in this treatise of Plotinus. Among these is a passage in the eighth book of the *Confessions* which discusses the flight of the soul in imitation of Plotinus but with some notable differences. Augustine, for example, omits the reference to Odysseus as a symbol of the soul's flight from this world, and, after dispensing with the ordinary modes of travel for this kind of flight, just as Plotinus does, he introduces the faculty of will (*voluntas*) where the problem for Plotinus was one of seeing (ὄψις).[83] We must indeed agree with Father Henry's emphasis on the importance of the will for Augustine; in the sentence in question it is repeated in such a way that there can be no room for misunderstanding. For in regard to the goal he was seeking, he tells us of the scene in the garden, to go in that direction and even to arrive there required only that he have the will to go, but a will that was vigorous and whole, not what was in fact a half-wounded will, tossing this way and that, divided in the struggle of one part with another.

In the course of time researches continued on the relation of Augustine to Plotinus and other predecessors, and in 1950 Courcelle, who has on many occasions illuminated the text of Augustine with his careful studies, pointed out that not only in the eighth but also in the first book of the *Confessions* Augustine employs the Plotinian passage regarding the flight of the soul. He had also discovered that the two passages from the *Confessions* and others as well in Augustine show a close similarity to some sermons of Ambrose for which Plotinus was clearly a model, and he came to the conclusion that Augustine in his early reading of Plotinus read him in the light of Ambrose's paraphrase. With regard to Augustine's omission of any reference to Odysseus, Courcelle finds this true also of Ambrose's treatment of the Plotinian passage

in his sermon *On Isaac or the soul,* which Augustine
may have heard in 386; but in the first book of the
Confessions he notes that Augustine adapts the passage of Plotinus to the parable of the prodigal son.[84]
What we might add is that Augustine's discussion of
the problem he found in his own will is not in his
Ambrosian model any more than it is in Plotinus.
Ambrose, following the lead of Plotinus, says that the
flight cannot be made on foot, and so on, but should
be made with the mind and indeed, he adds rather
quaintly, with the inner eyes or feet. Where Augustine
says that his will should be vigorous and whole (*velle
fortiter et integre*), Ambrose applies similar words to
seeing (*sanus et vigens oculus*), just as Plotinus does;[85]
and in the whole passage of Ambrose, which abounds
in allusions to vision, there is not one mention of the
will.[86]

From all this it might seem that Augustine, despite
any indebtedness he may have to Plotinus and Ambrose, is original in two respects: He substitutes the
prodigal son for Odysseus, the fabled wanderer of
pagan literature,[87] and he replaces seeing the good or
the beautiful with willing it. These two points, in fact,
could easily be understood as specifically Augustinian
contributions to the now old tradition of the soul's
flight. Augustine's fondness for the parable of the
prodigal son, allusions to which are scattered through
the *Confessions,* is readily explained by the events of
his life as they are recounted in this work; and the
reason in large measure for these experiences of his
was not any deficiency of knowing, as he analyzed his
own inner life, but one of willing. It is very difficult,

however, to ascribe originality to someone in matters of this kind, since we can never be sure of many of the elements involved in his intellectual and moral history, even when he reports them to us with the studiousness of an Augustine. In this instance I should like to suggest that Augustine is not the first to interject the parable of the prodigal son or the problem of the will into a discussion of the flight of the soul, and he is not original in this respect, at least in the way in which originality might commonly be understood. On both of these points he has been anticipated by Gregory of Nyssa.

3. The Flight of the Soul in Gregory of Nyssa

In a series of homilies *On the Lord's Prayer,* written at an unknown date but perhaps not many years before Augustine wrote the *Confessions,* Gregory, discoursing on the words, "Our Father, who art in heaven," discusses at some length the parable of the prodigal son both literally and in a figurative way. Just as in the parable, he says, it is the return of the son to the paternal hearth that occasions the benevolence of the father, so the Lord's Prayer, when it teaches us that the Father in heaven is called upon, seems to be reminding us of our beloved fatherland and to set us on the road that leads back to that fatherland. But the road leading human nature to heaven is nothing else than a flight from the evils of this earth, and the only means of making this flight is to become like God, which is to become just and holy and good. If anyone impresses these virtues clearly upon himself, as far as this is possible, then he will change effortlessly and spontaneously from an earthly to a heavenly existence. For the distance from the human to the divine is not one of space, so as to require some device by which to transfer this heavy and earthy flesh to an immaterial and spiritual manner of life. But rather, since the distance between virtue and vice is an intelligible one, it lies in man's will alone to take him to any place to which his desire is directed. Since there is no toil attached to choosing the good, and the choice leads at once to the attainment of what was chosen, it lies in our power to be in heaven immediately by holding God in our thought. When we are bidden, therefore, to call God our Father, this is nothing else than a command to become like our heavenly Father through a God-befitting mode of life.[88]

This last sentence of Gregory is a good example of the way in which Greek philosophical doctrines were employed to interpret the scriptural legacy of Christianity. There was nothing more natural to someone with his thorough training in Greek philosophy than to use the teachings which had become second nature to him to analyze the text of a scriptural passage like the Lord's Prayer and find there implications that are not at all obvious at first glance; and the same could be said of Augustine. Here Gregory is making use of the flight from the evils of this earth set forth in Plato's *Theaetetus,* the flight that consists in becoming like God, that is to say, in acquiring the various virtues that are enumerated; and the recollection that the prayer arouses in us likewise has a Platonic basis. But it is clear that all this comes to Gregory more immediately from Plotinus. There is the return to the fatherland, a characteristically Plotinian expression (though "fatherland" in a similar sense appears in Hebrews 11. 14). The flight we are speaking of is not in any way spatial, so that we do not have to find any device ($\mu\eta\chi\alpha\nu\dot{\eta}$) by which to accomplish it. As a result Gregory tends to look at the flight, at least in part, in the intellectual manner of Plotinus. We have only to grasp God in our thought in order to be spontaneously and without further effort transported to heaven. Yet there is more for Gregory than the intellect involved in this thought. There is an act of will, a choice to be made ($\pi\rho o\alpha\acute{\iota}\rho\epsilon\sigma\iota s$), and it lies within our power ($\acute{\epsilon}\xi\epsilon\sigma\tau\iota$) whether our thought will take us heavenward or leave us amid the evils of the world.

Gregory therefore introduces will or choice into the traditional flight of the soul, a notion that is absent from the corresponding passages of Plotinus and Ambrose, but turns up later in Augustine. It should be noted, however, that the element of will is not entirely lacking in Plotinus, as when he says elsewhere (5. 5. 12) that the Good is present as one wills it to be ($\dot{\omega}s\ \dot{\epsilon}\theta\acute{\epsilon}\lambda\epsilon\iota\ \tau\iota s$). What a difference there is, however, between their conception of will, whose choice of the good is followed at once by the attainment of it, and will as seen by Augustine, which has experienced the constant frustration of its choice because it could not come to a satisfactory agreement within itself as to what that choice should be! Now it would be unfair both to Gregory and to Plotinus to leave the impression that life for them is completely without difficulty and struggle. Both of them insist elsewhere that toil ($\pi\acute{o}\nu os$) is necessary for the acquisition of virtue,[89] and it is this, after all, that constitutes the flight of the soul for them, as it does earlier for Plato. One must admit, on the one hand, that there is considerable basis for the statements of Father Henry when he contrasts the proud rationalism of Plotinus, who has only to close his eyes to the outside world and awaken a sleeping power within himself, and the almost anguished Christianity of Augustine, who must bend his will under the yoke, and break the resistance of a nature that is wounded and divided against itself before he can win the struggle.[90] Yet, on the other hand, if we look at the larger picture presented by Plotinus, there are indications that he was not unaware of the serious problems involved in moral progress; and this is even truer of Gregory. But the fact is that in presenting their versions of the flight of the soul, whether this is understood as seeing or as willing, they have not touched on the real difficulties as an Augustine would see them. This is not an isolated instance in their philosophies, since they do not offer anywhere his kind of approach to the role played by the will in spiritual progress. But that is in itself a large topic that we cannot take into account here.

4. Development within Augustine's Thought

A word might be said of the difference to be found in Augustine's treatment of the flight of the soul at various periods of his life. In an early work, the *Soliloquies,* written about the time of his baptism, he says that there is more than one road (*via*) to wisdom (a view that he corrects in the *Retractations* 1. 4. 3, where he states that there is only one way, since Christ has said, "I am the way."). Each person is able, he says, to take hold of wisdom according to his own health and vigor (*sanitate ac firmitate*), and, describing it as a kind of light, he goes on to speak of it in terms of sight and the sun (1. 13. 23). We should flee utterly from sensible things;[91] we have need of wings that are whole and perfect (*integris perfectisque*) in order to fly[92] to that light out of the darkness in which we now live (1. 14. 24). Just as the bodily eye cannot look upon the sun unless it is healthy (*sanus*), so it is with the soul, which is often deceived regarding its own health (1. 14. 25). This intellectual interpretation of the soul's flight is found also in the work *Against the Academics,* written in the same period. The soul, he says, expects to overcome all deception and, by grasping the truth and returning, as it were, to its place of origin (*quasi in regionem suae originis rediens*), to triumph over the passions; it expects thus that by espousing temperance it will be the ruler, and it is less concerned about its return to heaven (*securior rediturus in coelum*) (2. 9. 22).[93] (In the *Retractations* 1. 1. 3 Augustine says that it would have been safer to speak of going (*iturus*) than of returning (*rediturus*) to heaven, since in this way he would not have given the impression of accepting the doctrine that the soul, having fallen or been cast down from heaven because of its sins, has been thrust into the body.)[94]

In the first book of his work *On Christian doctrine,* written about ten years later, we see a shift from this highly intellectual approach to the flight of the soul. Speaking of those who ask how one knows that the unchangeably wise life is to be placed ahead of that which is changeable, he says that the one who does not see this is like the blind man in the full light of the sun, while the one who sees the answer to this question but runs away from it has a spiritual vision that has been blunted by the continued presence of shadows arising from the flesh. Men are therefore driven away from their very fatherland by what we might call the contrary winds of corrupt habits; they pursue the lower though they recognize that there is something higher (1. 9. 9). If one is going to enjoy the unchanging truth, the soul must be purified so as to be able to see that light and, once seen, cleave to it. This purification should be thought of as a kind of walking or sailing toward the fatherland; to Him who is everywhere present we do not move by change of place, but by good inclination (*studio*) and good habits (1. 10. 10).[95] Here Augustine, though retaining a basically intellectual interpretation of the soul's flight, sets clearly apart those men who see the light but abandon it. He recognizes that through moral depravity a man may pursue what he knows to be inferior, and that to move toward the fatherland is a matter of inclination and character. This tendency toward a moral interpretation of the soul's flight points to the *Confessions,* written probably not much later, and it is in the *Confessions* that the problem of the will comes to the fore.

Finally, we may look at two passages written at a still later date. In the first of these (*Enarr. in Ps. CXLIX* 5) Augustine says that the fatherland is to be approached through love, not with bodily feet. Ships are not required, but the two wings of charity, namely, love of God and love of neighbor. This definitely non-intellectual interpretation of the flight of the soul adopted by Augustine in his maturity is supplemented by a passage from the *City of God* (9. 17), in which Plotinus is quoted by name. We must flee, then, says Augustine, to the most beloved fatherland. There is the Father, and there is everything. What kind of fleet (*classis*) can we employ, what means of flight (*fuga*)? To become like God. Augustine goes on to say that the only distance from God is unlikeness to Him, and the soul is more unlike the eternal and the unchangeable the more it seeks after temporal and changing things. To heal this illness—since the mortal and impure found in the lowest cannot fittingly belong (*convenire non possunt*) to the immortal purity that is in the highest—there is need of a mediator. This mediator cannot have a diseased mind such as belongs to those on the lowest level, for then he would through envy begrudge our being healed instead of helping us to be healed. But he must, by the immortal justice of the spirit, through which he remains on the highest level—not by spatial distance (*locorum distantia*), but by the excellence of likeness—offer truly divine aid for our purification and liberation.

From the period of the *Soliloquies* and *Against the Academics* to that of the work *On Christian doctrine* and especially the *Confessions* there is a definite change to be observed in Augustine's treatment of the flight of the soul. His earliest interpretation is set forth in the intellectual terms favored by Plotinus and Ambrose, but the later one turns from the conception of the flight as a vision to a consideration of the will's function in making the journey. We cannot easily think that the reason for the change in Augustine's attitude lay primarily in the events themselves which he interprets for us in the *Confessions,* since these events, at least those that are relevant, had already taken place when he wrote the two earlier works. The reason is rather to be sought in the mental development that occurred in the intervening time, as a result of which he came to apply the theme of the flight in a very personal way to his own life, and especially to the problems, which he analyzed with great care and clarity, of his will. In this process was Augustine aided or inspired by anything he read or heard of during these years? If we are guided by his earlier treatment of the flight, and by what we know of his method of writing in general, it is easy to believe that there were various influences operating in his life which he used in his own way. The passage of Gregory discussed above offers itself as one possibility—even though at this moment there is no historical evidence that Augustine had any contact with it—since it brings together in a very natural way a number of features that turn up in Augustine's later handling of the flight of the soul.

5. Augustine and Gregory of Nyssa Compared

Most noteworthy perhaps of these is the employment, in the first book of the *Confessions* (1. 18. 28), of the parable of the prodigal son in connection with the ancient theme. The entrance of the prodigal son into Gregory's exegesis of the Lord's Prayer is most appropriate, since the words uttered by the wayward youth regarding his sin against heaven and against his father have a ready association with the opening of the prayer, and both of these in turn suggest the traditional fatherland and the return that consists in becoming like God. A conception like that of the prodigal son is found also in Plotinus,[96] and it is not unlikely that Gregory's acquaintance with Plotinus suggested to him the use of the scriptural counterpart. In Augustine, on the other hand, the Plotinian theme of the flight is employed to express, not the return to God, but his distance from God at the time; and there are other notions from the same passage of Plotinus in the preceding context of Augustine: the bottomless abyss (*inmanissimo profundo*) and the darkness of ignoble desire (*affectu tenebroso*). The prodigal son enters only in the midst of the enumeration of the possible ways of approaching or leaving God. Having said that not on foot or by any spatial distance does anyone leave God or return to Him, he adds that the prodigal son (*filius ille tuus minor*) did not seek horses, and so on, for his departure. Augustine has not so much adapted the theme of flight to the parable of the prodigal son, as Courcelle describes it,[97] as he has fitted the prodigal son into the flight, making him the substitute for Odysseus. Now such a substitution would not be very difficult for a Christian writer of some imagination. But the fact is that an association between the prodigal son and the flight of the soul had already been made by at least one predecessor of

Augustine, and in a way, one might add, that arises most naturally out of the whole context. In Augustine, on the other hand, there seems to be no strong motivation of an intrinsic nature for the introduction of the prodigal son at this particular place. In fact, his arrival on the scene is abrupt and his presence rather casual. The earthly father is not mentioned because he is merged with the heavenly Father, who is addressed by Augustine as the kind Father who had been generous to the youth on his setting out and a kinder Father when he returned in his hour of need. This easy merging of the two fathers suggests that Augustine has in mind a passage, such as that of Gregory, in which the merging is more careful and deliberate, one in which the kindness of the father on the return of the son is emphasized, as indeed it is at some length in Gregory.

One further point is worth mentioning in this passage of Augustine. When he says that the departure from God and the return to Him are not by any spatial distances (*spatiis locorum*), he is using an expression that does not have a close equivalent in any passage of Plotinus involving the flight of the soul. There are, to be sure, other ways in which Plotinus can indicate this. In the treatise we have been discussing the very dismissal of the ordinary forms of travel indicates that no spatial separation is involved (1. 6. 8); and in the following chapter he states that the true light has no magnitude ($\mu\acute{\epsilon}\gamma\epsilon\theta$os). He makes a more explicit statement in another treatise (1. 8. 7), where he is interpreting the Platonic flight of the soul. Plato says, according to Plotinus, that the flight is not spatial (τόπῳ; the phrase is really the addition of Plotinus), but comes about by the acquisition of virtue and by separating oneself from the body. It is interesting to note, however, that in the passage of Gregory we find the expression, "spatial distance" (τοπικὴ διάστασις), which is closer than anything in Plotinus to Augustine's way of putting it, to which I shall return shortly.

In one passage of the *Confessions* that refers to the flight of the soul, though not to the prodigal son, Augustine distinguishes between "presumption" and "confession": On the one side are those men who see where one should go without seeing by which way; on the other side is the way that leads to the beatific fatherland, and not merely to be seen but also to be lived in (7. 20. 26).[98] In speaking of "the way that leads to the beatific fatherland" (*viam ducentem ad beatificam patriam*) Augustine comes very close to an expression used by Gregory, "the road leading back to the fatherland" (τῇ ὁδῷ τῇ πρὸς τὴν πατρίδα πάλιν ἐπαναγούσῃ); a little earlier in the same sentence "fatherland" is qualified by "good" (ἀγαθῆς πατρίδος).

In a later passage of the *Confessions* (8. 8. 19), which we have already discussed, there is another interesting resemblance to the passage of Gregory. After dismissing three ways of making the flight Augustine says that not only to go but also to arrive at his destination was nothing else than (*nihil erat aliud quam*) to will to go. The phrasing, which does not occur in the corresponding passage of Plotinus, is to be found three times in Gregory: the road leading to heaven is none other than (οὐδεμία τίς ἐστιν ἄλλη εἰ

65

μή) a flight; the means of making the flight seems to him none other than (οὐκ ἄλλη μοί τις εἶναι δοκεῖ πλήν) becoming like God; and the command to call God Father is nothing else than (οὐδὲν ἔτερον ἤ) one that bids us to become like the heavenly Father. This similarity of terminology would not be worthy of mention as an isolated phenomenon, but it also represents a survival in Augustine of the view, quite natural in Plotinus and Gregory, that there is no "toil" attached to the flight of the soul, and no means of physical transport need be prepared.[99] Augustine too sees that he has no need to look for bodily transportation. But he is brought close to the verge of a discrepancy, since by introducing his conception of will, especially in the graphic terms he goes on to employ in the following paragraphs (8. 8. 19–9. 21), he makes it clear that for him the greatest "toil" is involved precisely because it *is* a question of will. Yet in this near discrepancy there is a touch of irony that is not lacking in rhetorical skill. I should add that the section of Ambrose's sermon, *On Isaac or the soul,* to which Courcelle calls attention in pointing out resemblances of Augustine to Ambrose does not contain such an expression, any more than it does a reference to "spatial distance" or to "the road leading to the fatherland," or, above all, any suggestion of the prodigal son.

The employment of historical data to explain differences, or seeming differences, in the doctrines a philosopher has written at various times is a procedure that is readily open to abuse and must be undertaken with caution. Yet it is tempting to think that if Augustine, in the years that intervened between the earlier works already mentioned and the *Confessions,* came across in some way a treatment of the flight of the soul such as that of Gregory, it would help to explain the particular way in which he introduces the parable of the prodigal son in the later work. Once introduced the parable is referred to often, not at length or very explicitly, but in a way that strongly suggests it is not far from his thoughts about himself.[100] If we turn to the passage of the *City of God* (9. 17) in which we saw Augustine quoting Plotinus on the flight of the soul, there are two features worth looking at. First, the mediator is said to remain on the highest level, but "not by spatial distance" (*locorum distantia*). We noted that Augustine (*Conf.* 1. 18. 28) uses a very similar expression (*spatiis locorum*) in order to state that this is not the way in which we depart from God and return to Him, just before he introduces the prodigal son. Both expressions are very much like the one of Gregory (τοπικὴ διάστασις), that of the *City of God* being as close to a literal translation as good Latin usage would permit. In the second place, Augustine, though ostensibly quoting Plotinus, answers the question regarding the mode of flight by saying that it consists in becoming like God. This is not the answer that Plotinus gives in this place, although, of course, he makes use of this Platonic expression elsewhere, and, in particular, he has just used it two chapters earlier in this same treatise (1. 6. 6). Nor should we overlook the beginning of another treatise (1. 2. 1), where Plotinus, quoting Plato's *Theaetetus,* answers the question about the flight from this world in the same way as Augustine does here. Courcelle suggests that, as opposed to the passage Augustine paraphrases from Plotinus, in Ambrose the conclusion of the argument is, in fact: "Let us make ourselves like the Good."[101] While the Good to which Ambrose refers is naturally God, there is actually a closer correspondence in this respect with the passage of Gregory, for whom the flight consists explicitly in becoming like God.[102]

The hypothesis that Augustine, during the years that preceded the writing of the *Confessions,* was in some way influenced by Gregory's discussion of the prodigal son, or another like it, serves to explain a number of features, otherwise difficult to account for, in Augustine's treatment of the flight of the soul and the parable of the prodigal son. In the one passage of Gregory are brought together a not inconsiderable number of elements that Augustine employs in reference to these two themes from about the period when he wrote the *Confessions.* Above all is the fact that Gregory joins the Platonic admonition of flight from this world—and becoming like God—as adapted by Plotinus to the soul's flight to the fatherland, to the parable of the prodigal son, this too perhaps suggested by Plotinus himself, but in other places. Then there is the introduction by Gregory of the notion of willing, partly in addition to, and partly in substitution for, that of seeing in the Plotinian flight; this is a most important step in the direction of Augustine's treatment of the will's role in his going towards God. As for the minor resemblances between Augustine and Gregory, such as the denial of "spatial distance" between man and God, "the road leading to the fatherland," and the absence of "toil" in making the flight, these represent themes found in the single passage of Gregory that have been assembled from various treatises of Plotinus but adapted in such a way and expressed in such a terminology that it might seem to be Gregory rather than Plotinus who is echoed in Augustine.

In making these comparisons between Augustine and Gregory I do not mean to suggest that Augustine must have known this or that passage in his predecessor either directly or through an intermediary. The search for the historical and literary influences in Augustine's life is very complex, and at this point we can only say that a beginning has been made to ascertain what they were. The difficulty is not merely in the many gaps that exist in our knowledge of his sources, many of which will doubtless be filled as time goes on. It is also in the manner in which Augustine uses these sources. Even when Plotinus, for example, is quoted by name, there is no guarantee that the text itself at that moment is before Augustine's eyes. He doubtless knew many texts of Plotinus and others quite well. But his recollection of those texts and the use he makes of them are affected by other texts and other associations, just as Courcelle finds is true of Ambrose's interpretations of Plotinus.[103] But, more than this, we know that we are dealing with a mind that was not only eager and retentive but always extremely active in applying the knowledge it had acquired to the problem of the moment, and in adapting that knowledge to suit the problem itself rather than the source from which it came. Few certainties await the one who seeks the precise sources of Augustine's thought, and even the probabilities are all too readily subject to revision. If we were to ask whether Augustine himself could have been responsible for those features of his adaptation of the soul's flight that in point of time were actually anticipated by Gregory, the answer would have to be affirmative. This seems to me, however, extremely unlikely, and I think there must have been one or more still undetermined sources that influenced in an important way his treatment of this theme. To those who may find further evidence on this point, corroborative or otherwise, I suggest the name of Gregory of Nyssa as a possible source—direct or indirect—of this feature of Augustine's thought.

6. Distinctive Features of Augustine's Treatment

But to most of us assembled here today such interests, fascinating as they can be, are not the chief reason for studying Augustine. Even if we were able to determine precisely the elements of a given question that he had received from his predecessors—and I think that for these elements he is very much indebted to others—it is just at this point that we begin to see Augustine himself. Suppose that we were to admit for the moment that the fusion of the soul's flight with the parable of the prodigal son, along with such other details as I have mentioned, was really inspired by the passage of Gregory or something very much like it. What could we say is specifically Augustinian in the passage where this occurs? Though this type of analysis could be endless, we can look at a few of the more obvious features. We would notice first, I suppose, the very personal orientation of the entire context. Augustine himself is the soul whom God draws out of the bottomless abyss, the one who cries out, "I have sought Your face, O Lord!" He is the one who is far from the face of the Lord in the darkness of ignoble desire. The word "far" suggests, by association, that it is not on foot or by any spatial distance that one departs from God or returns to Him. Here Augustine has added the notion of departure to the formula of transport, which in Plotinus, Gregory, and Ambrose is employed only for the return of the soul to God. There is certainly a basis for this in Plotinus' thought as a whole, but Augustine, to make the formula itself more directly applicable to his position at the time with reference to God, expands it to include departure as well as return. The formula is continued but shifted now to the prodigal son, so that it is clear that Augustine identifies himself with the youth who went on his journey without benefit of such means as horses and ships. The substance he wasted while living in the far-off land was given to him by his heavenly Father. We have seen that for Gregory the heavenly Father is symbolized by the youth's earthly father. But Augustine, by bringing in the heavenly Father without any reference to the earthly one, and by addressing Him in the second person, makes Him more pointedly the kind Father of himself as well, and one from whom even greater kindness can be expected on his return.

Even though we were to admit that all the elements employed by Augustine in these few lines have been received by him from one source or another, and even if our knowledge of the sources should be ten times greater than it is today, his true originality would always stand out. He has chosen from all the traditional materials available to him those that are most directly relevant to a concretely visualized situation, one in which he is inevitably at the center, and he adapts them to his own person with such a clear understanding of his human condition that he readily becomes a symbol of universal humanity. Thus from an historical or a philological point of view the parable of the prodigal son may be said to enter the discussions of Gregory more smoothly and naturally. But considered as a philosophical device it is Augustine who weaves it with greater effect into his discourse, because he has already woven it into his own life and into the life of man.

We have noted, in somewhat different terms, how this personal orientation affects his treatment of the will in making the flight to God. For Plato the flight from the evils of this world, that is, becoming like God, is employed as a dialectical device to communicate something of the different standards of value employed by men. Within the relatively rigid hierarchical system of Plotinus the flight becomes explicitly the ascent of the soul to the higher levels of perfection through the awakening of its intellectual power of seeing. In Gregory of Nyssa will or choice ($\pi\rho oa\iota\rho\epsilon\sigma\iota\varsigma$) replaces vision ($\delta\psi\iota\varsigma$), but there is no suggestion that this substitution raises serious moral problems, since choice, as he describes it, is as far removed from the notion of "toil" as the vision that Plotinus associates with his flight of the soul. When Augustine, however, introduces "will" (*voluntas*), in his sense of the term, into the traditional framework, the flight to God takes on an entirely new meaning. He discovers from his own experiences, and especially from his introspection on these experiences, that willing does not automatically lead to the action that has been willed, since the will may be divided against itself in a bitter struggle and therefore unable to perform its function with the wholeness that Gregory doubtless has in mind. Augustine's detailed analysis of the way in which a will acts, which forms part of the passage in the eighth book of the *Confessions* (8. 8. 19–9. 21) employing the theme of flight, with his description of the way in which his limbs obeyed the slightest movement of his soul's will more readily than the soul obeyed itself in carrying out its own will within the will alone—all this manifests, within the inherited framework, a new conception of the flight to God, one that arises in a very immediate way out of the experiences of life itself.

Father Henry, in his fine analysis of the differences that set Augustine apart from Plotinus in the passages that show most clearly the influence of the Neo-Platonist, states that for the one it is sufficient to see, while for the other it is necessary to will, and that Plotinus and Augustine are separated by the Christian dogma of original sin.[104] While this evaluation is certainly true regarding these two men, we might wonder what to do if we tried to distinguish Augustine from Gregory. Gregory agrees with Augustine that original sin is to be taken into account, and he is just as familiar as Augustine is, at least on the theoretical level, with the Christian doctrine of divine grace and St. Paul's teaching on divided man who can fail in what he wills (Rom. 7. 15). Yet, though he too replaces the Plotinian vision with willing in the flight to God, in many ways his conception of the flight remains closer to that of Plotinus, however much the basic spirit is genuinely Christian. It is here that the originality of Augustine becomes even clearer, since we can compare him, not with a pagan philosopher, but with a thinker whose religious views—along with a generally similar philosophical tradition—he shares. It is often, in fact, the very closeness of their doctrines, of which the use of the will in interpreting the flight to God is an example, that serves as a background for the strength and vitality manifested by Augustine's more personal and introspective approach to the traditional problems.

III. Time and the Soul

1. The Relation of Time to Soul in Greek Thought to Plotinus

Augustine's new and more personally oriented conception of the flight to God is only one aspect of what has been called in him and in other thinkers, coming even to the present time, the philosophy of "interiority."[105] That part of Augustine's "interiority" which has probably had the greatest influence on his successors is the theory of time he developed by introspection into the life of his soul. Here again he was not without predecessors from whom he received a good deal. But the manner in which he utilized these materials and created something distinctively new is the best possible illustration of where his true originality is to be found.

An explanation of time from the psychological point of view does not occur very early in Greek thought, although it is more or less clearly suggested in various discussions that approach the problem differently. Plato, looking on time as a principle of regularity and order in the universe, calls it an image of eternity, one that proceeds according to number in imitation of eternity that abides in unity.[106] This description certainly does not seem in any way psychological. But if the number according to which time proceeds, that by virtue of which there is order in the universe, has any meaning, that can only be with reference to a mind in which one member of a numerical series is seen in relation to those before and after it. A similar statement could be made of Aristotle's definition of time as the number or measure of motion, however much his very literal account may otherwise differ from the metaphorical one of Plato.[107] In Aristotle's narrowly restricted analysis of the relation of time to physical motion the psychological significance of time has no place. Yet he admits, though only in a passing comment, that without a mind to do the numbering there would be no such number as time.[108] It is interesting to speculate what Aristotle might have said of time in a treatise in which he considered the psychological aspect relevant and gave it his full attention. We are perhaps given a slight indication of what this might be by a passage in his *Rhetoric* (2. 12. 8), in which he is speaking of some of the characteristics of the young. They live for the most part, he says, in expectation. For expectation (ἐλπίς) is concerned with the future, memory (μνήμη) with the past; and to the young the future is long, the past short. At the beginning of life there is nothing to be remembered, everything to be expected. Aristotle here, though he offers no formal treatment of time, shows once more that he is aware of some of its psychological implications, and he employs two terms, memory and expectation, that later have considerable importance in the treatment of time by Augustine.[109]

In the transfer of time from the physical realm of Aristotle to the psychological one of Augustine a more important role is played by Plotinus than might at first seem likely. Although Plotinus, partly on the basis of some Platonic passages, especially in the *Timaeus,* places time in the soul, this does not mean at all what such an expression will later mean to Augustine.[110] Plotinus is not speaking of the consciousness or calculation of time within the individual human soul, but rather the creation, by a universal principle called soul, of the world and all it contains, and time is identified by him with the creative life of this principle. Time is therefore said to be in soul as the vital power by which soul creates, and the universe with all its motion, existing as it does within this life, is in time. Far from being a number or measure of motion, as time was for Aristotle and will be, in a different way, for Augustine, time for Plotinus is the power that is presupposed in all motion as its cause. Even when he speaks of time as existing in human souls, this has a metaphysical rather than a psychological significance, since here too time is not the measure but the cause of the motions of men. To express the relation of time to soul Plotinus says that it is a distention—or extension—of the life of soul (διάστασις ζωῆς). This does not mean, however, that in soul as such there is any succession of creative stages corresponding to those in the motions produced by it. Soul, as one of Plotinus' three divine principles, albeit the lowest, is above all succession or distention. But the term "distention" may be applied to it metaphorically, in the sense that, remaining ever without distention in itself, it has in its total life a creative aspect that is responsible for a universe in which real distention appears.[111] Because of the position occupied by soul in Plotinus' hierarchy, midway as it is between the higher principles and the sensible universe, Plotinus refers to it in one place as an "inextended extension" (διάστημα ἀδιάστατον).[112]

2. The Nature of Time in Gregory of Nyssa

The view that time is a kind of distention receives some new—and perhaps unexpected—variations in the works of Gregory of Nyssa. From one point of view time for him is closely connected with place and other components of the universe; in particular, time and place are produced by God as a kind of receptacle in which all things are created.[113] He is following here Plato's *Timaeus* (52B), though for Plato only space is described as a receptacle for becoming. For Gregory time may likewise be defined as a distention (διάστημα) accompanying or running along with the universe of becoming, the position of the Stoic Chrysippus; but he may also call it the measure of all motion in the universe, an echo of Aristotle.[114] Although time is only one aspect of the distention that distinguishes the creature from the Creator, it becomes an especially significant one in Gregory's insistence on the absence of temporal sequence in the nature of God and in the generation of the second person of the Trinity. Such discussions come, quite naturally, to involve a close consideration of the life of God, and to contrast this life with the life that is best known to us, human life. Gregory, following the emphasis of Plotinus, refers eternity, the absence of all temporal distention, chiefly to God's *life*, with the result that time also, by way of contrast to eternity, is referred in a special manner to human life, and above all to the intellectual activity in which man manifests the greatest likeness to the life of God. In this process the influence of Plotinus can be seen also in the way in which Gregory, in contrasting eternity and time as two forms of life, distinguishes them by the application of various pairs of contraries to the basic notion of life. Thus, though Gregory employs the old Stoic term for "distention" (διάστημα) rather than the Plotinian (διάστασις) in reference to time, and even echoes some of the Stoic phraseology, he is more clearly in the tradition of Plato and Plotinus. Time for him tends in the direction of being understood as a form of life, but with Plotinus' universal principle of soul eliminated, since he could not accept this. As a result time is transferred to the only soul available, that of man. But here time cannot have the function of a creative power, as it does in Plotinus. The time that is relevant to the human soul does not create the motions of man. It exists rather in his mind through the powers of memory and expectation, and it both distinguishes him from God as a creature leading a divided life and offers him the means to make his way through this life in order to reach a higher one.

It might be worth while to look briefly at one passage in which Gregory makes the contrast between the two kinds of life, the divine and the human. The divine nature, he says, is self-sufficient, eternal, and all-embracing; and it is before and above such marks of the world of becoming as place and time. This nature cannot be measured by temporal periods or run along with the course of time, but, being firmly fixed in itself, it is not divided into past and future. For past and future are affections ($\pi\acute{a}\theta\eta$) proper to created beings, and they refer to the memory and expectation of the life that is divided by time. But for that lofty and blessed being, to which all things are eternally present, both the past and that which is expected are dominated by its all-embracing power.[115]

In this passage we note that past and future, which are naturally said to characterize created beings, since these are set off from the Creator by the mark of "distention," are applied in a particular way to the distention of life, and clearly human life, since it is this life that is divided, not merely by past and future, as other created things are, but by past and future interpreted in a psychological sense, that is, by memory and expectation. The equivalence for Gregory of memory and expectation to past and future in such a context is confirmed by the sentence in which, denying that in God's eternal present there is any room for the past and the future, he says that the past and the *expected* are dominated by His power.

Thus time for Gregory, which begins, one might say, by being a single aspect of the distention that distinguishes all creatures from the Creator, ends by becoming a special mark of human life. In contrast to eternity, which is the living present of God, time is the division that is proper to man, going beyond the simple division of past and future that is found elsewhere in creation, and reaching his highest and most distinctive powers, so that here too, and in a very special manner, through the division of his life into memory and expectation, he bears the mark of the creature. Though time is found everywhere in this sensible universe, it has a unique significance in the life of man, since he does not merely participate in the general flux of becoming, but he alone possesses a spiritual power of projecting himself into the past and the future, which come thus to be equated with memory and expectation as manifestations of the soul's divided life. It is not difficult for Gregory then to consider human life not merely a distention in the metaphysical sense, but also, in a moral sense, a distraction, as we are told in the words of Ecclesiastes.[116] Both the distention and the distraction will be completely overcome only in the future life, when the soul, stripped of emotion and having become like God, will no longer have a place for expectation or memory. For it will possess at last the object of its expectation, and the enjoyment of the good that is present will cast out all memory.[117]

Augustine is not the first, therefore, to devise a psychological theory of time. Gregory had already done this, but by a method that is very different from the introspective approach that Augustine will shortly employ. Gregory has taken a number of inherited views, generally metaphysical and cosmological, regarding the nature of time, and has turned them in a direction that leads very naturally to the realm of the psychological. This is part of a larger tendency in the cosmology of Greek Christianity to look upon the universe in an anthropocentric way, since, according to the Christian view of divine providence, the universe cannot be understood in isolation from the pilgrimage that man must undertake in it to gain his salvation. Basil of Caesarea, the brother of Gregory, expresses this attitude towards the universe succinctly in calling it a "training school for rational souls."[118] Since the universe, therefore, has been created by God for the sake of man, cosmology cannot be studied adequately in isolation from anthropology or from the history of man on earth. But Gregory goes significantly beyond his predecessors and contemporaries in perceiving that a theory of time should be adapted to the central position of man in the universal scheme. Though possessing the mark of "distention" in common with created things, man must fashion his own destiny in a special way, so that he must be conscious of his position in the universe and, in particular, of the divided life that he possesses. Thus the universal distention rises to the level of self-consciousness in man, and a metaphysical time becomes psychological.[119]

3. The Psychological Approach of Augustine

When Augustine approaches the problem of time in the eleventh book of the *Confessions,* where we find his most distinctive treatment of the subject, his larger purpose in doing this is to show that the universe is in time, while God is in eternity.[120] Though such an occasion might suggest a view of time that relates it closely to objectively existing motion, Augustine from the very beginning of his analysis makes it clear that, for the first time in the history of philosophy, the point of departure in the discussion of this traditional problem will be the data of introspection.

The difficulties with which Augustine introduces the question recall the passage in Aristotle's *Physics* at the beginning of his treatment of time, in which he wonders, for example, whether time even exists. For part of it has gone and no longer exists, while part is still to come and does not yet exist (the present moment is a dividing point between past and future, not a part such as can make up a whole); but a thing that is made up of non-existent parts can hardly be said to exist itself.[121] Though Aristotle doubtless thought that in his own discussion of time such difficulties as these were satisfactorily answered, opinion on this point was not unanimous. Not at all surprisingly, a dissenting voice is that of Sextus Empiricus, the sceptic who lived two hundred years before Augustine. In his works we read some of the same objections regarding the existence of time as Aristotle had formulated much earlier and appear later in Augustine's *Confessions*. He repeats Aristotle's statement that anything composed of non-existents will not exist, and this can certainly be said of time, composed as it is of past and future.[122] Anticipating Augustine, but without in this instance having an exact precedent in Aristotle, Sextus attacks those who would say that the present day exists. For when we are in the first hour of the day, the other hours do not exist, so that one would have to maintain that a day exists even when most of its hours do not. But not even one hour exists, if we pursue the point, since an hour too is divisible into parts, and while one part exists the others do not.[123] An interesting objection Sextus makes to the existence of time, from Augustine's point of view, is that if someone (to justify time's existence) maintains that the past and future exist then both of these must exist in the present. But for the past and future to exist in the present would mean that they were in present time, which is absurd.[124]

Highly significant from the standpoint of Augustine is the interpretation given by Sextus to the Aristotelian definition of time. Paraphrasing it as the number of the prior and posterior in motion, he understands this to mean a sort of "recollection" (συμμνημόνευσις) of the prior and posterior in motion.[125] The fact that he substitutes "recollection" for "number" in his second paraphrase indicates that the Aristotelian position, which is intended to be strictly physical by relating time to motion and not to the mind, has been given a psychological interpretation that already foreshadows, in a very general way, the position of Augustine, in which also "recollection" has an important place. Some light may be thrown on the rare word that Sextus uses for "recollection" by a passage in which he describes the view of those who maintain that motion is perceived, not by sensation, but by the intellect through sensation, and who state that motion comes about in accordance with recollection (κατὰ συμμνημόνευσιν); for it is by recalling that this body was formerly in that place but is now in this that we form the conception of motion.[126] The more explicit doctrine described by Sextus with regard to motion suggests without difficulty how the notion of recollection is to be applied to Aristotle's theory of time, though Aristotle himself, whatever basis he may offer here and there for such an interpretation, carefully limits his analysis in the *Physics* to the relevance of time to nature itself.

Augustine, like Aristotle, and unlike a sceptic such as Sextus Empiricus, for whom the difficulties involved in the problem of time are accepted as a ground for denying its existence, finds in the very discussion of these difficulties a means of seeking a solution. With Augustine the dialectical analysis of the apparent paradoxes offered by our ordinary conception of time continues longer than Aristotle's and may be said to lead in a more continuous way to the ultimate solution he offers. In Aristotle the introspective approach, of which the writer is clearly not unaware, is limited to his preliminary discussion, and it is left behind when he comes to the formal analysis of time in terms of the principles that are proper to the study of nature.[127] In Augustine there is no such clear-cut distinction of the methods to be employed in different fields of knowledge, and as a result his analysis is able to proceed along the same introspective line on which he begins. For this reason the difficulties with which he opens his treatment of time find a more evident solution in his later, more positive, remarks about it than is the case with Aristotle.

Augustine's procedure is very empirical regarding what we actually think and say about time. Since we are able to measure longer and shorter periods of time, we must say that no time can be long unless it actually exists, unless, therefore, it is in some way present, since past and future do not as such exist. But it is difficult to see how a long time can be present, because the present has no extension at all. Instead of giving up at this point Augustine employs the paradox to help him find a solution. The analysis of his inner life tells him that when we measure a past event it is not the event itself that is measured but the image that the past event, which is no longer, has left in our memory;[128] so also we do not perceive a future event, since it does not exist, but can predict it from some present cause or sign that foreshadows it. We must thus hold, he says, contrary though it is to what we have been taught, that past and future events do not exist, and it is only a concession to popular custom to state that there *are* three times, past, present, and future. It would be more proper to say that there are three times, the present with reference to past events, the present with reference to present events, and the present with reference to future events. His analysis tells him that all three of these present times can be only in the mind, that is, a present memory of past events, a present attention to present events, and a present expectation of future events.[129]

Though he has made some progress up to this point, he has not yet found out what time really is; he now pauses, as it were, and takes a new direction. To the suggestion of a "learned man" that the motions of the sun, moon, and stars constitute "times" he says he could not agree, because even if all the heavenly motions should cease and a potter's wheel should continue to move there would be time by which the revolutions of the wheel could be measured. Moreover, there is the scriptural account of the sun's standing still while the victory was won. This battle was completed in a period of time that was sufficient for it even though the sun was not in motion. The example confirms his opinion that time is independent of the motions of the heavenly bodies, and it likewise suggests to him that time is some kind of distention (*distentio*), since the battle took place in time.[130]

This section of his argument is of considerable importance to Augustine's progress, since the concept of a distention enters into his eventual solution. I think that Augustine has written this portion of his text under the influence—perhaps only indirect—of a passage in Basil of Caesarea, who is there criticizing the Arian heretic Eunomius—the "learned man" of Augustine—for defining time in terms of the heavenly motions.[131] While he is dismissing this definition of time and looking for confirmation of his stand in the scriptural account of the battle, he comes to realize that time has something to do with motion[132] even if it does not depend on a particular motion. Up to this point his analysis of time has been almost purely psychological, with little reference to motion. But now, in the act of distinguishing time from motion, he is able to refer time to motion in such a way as to call it a distention. As a result the three functions of the mind which he spoke of earlier, memory, attention, and expectation, may be considered no longer discrete activities but rather three aspects of a single distention; this distention, as further psychological analysis makes clear, must be one of the mind distending itself into the past and the future in order to measure motion.[133] Thus Augustine's view, which has a point of departure that is completely psychological, is made more precise by being given a non-psychological reference, and these results are confirmed and extended by additional psychological analysis.

4. Augustine and His Predecessors Compared

There is much similarity in this treatment of time to that of Aristotle, since Augustine too considers time a measure of motion and often uses statements about it that had been or could have been used by Aristotle as well. But everywhere we can observe a transference on Augustine's part from the physical to the psychological. The present moment, or the now, for Aristotle, since it is the existing phase of motion considered as numerable, is both a dividing point and a link between the past and the future. For Augustine, however, the now as the boundary of time is the mind's attention, for time itself exists only in the activity of the mind. As the now of Aristotle is the boundary between past and future, so in Augustine it is the mind's attention which is the boundary between memory and expectation; and time possesses its continuity in this attention of the mind because expectation must pass through attention in order to become memory. This link, however, between past and future cannot be considered quantitative for Augustine in the same way as it is for Aristotle. For the moment at which the mind reckons time must be indivisible, and all the other moments, past and future, that are included in the reckoning must be in the mind at this same indivisible moment. It is, in fact, by means of his psychological approach that Augustine meets head on the objections of a Sextus Empiricus, for whom past and future can be considered as existing only if they exist in the present, which seems to him absurd. Augustine accepts the statement that past and future coexist in the present and utilizes this apparent absurdity to arrive at a solution expressed in psychological terms. Time is therefore an activity of the mind for Augustine that possesses continuity but not in a strictly quantitative way, even though the motion measured by time is itself quantitative. For Aristotle time as the measure is quantitative, just as is the motion that is measured, while for Augustine it is not a quantity but a vital activity, to which quantitative terms may be applied with reference to the motion that is measured by it.

We can also perceive a resemblance, though of a

different kind, to Plotinus' theory of time. For Plotinus the life of soul considered in itself has no succession or distention, but time, since it is the creative activity of soul, is distended because of its reference to the motion it produces in the sensible universe. Augustine differs, of course, from Plotinus in that time for him is the measure rather than the cause of motion. But he agrees with his predecessor in making time consist in a vital activity of a soul, for him the human soul. Since motion can take place not all at once but only in succession, the mind represents this real succession and distention to itself by means of an activity that can be called a distention by analogy. Augustine might well have used here Plotinus' statement that soul is an "inextended extension."[134] Moreover, just as for Plotinus soul has a position lower than the life of eternity but higher than the universe, so the human soul for Augustine is between God and nature. The activity of mind identified with time by Augustine must be superior to the motion of nature in order to measure it, and it must stand as something relatively permanent above the flux and distention of this motion. This permanence is found in the "attention" of the soul, which is always present and as such always the same. But since man exists in a world of change to which he must adapt himself, not everything can be the object of his attention. In the motions around him there is constant succession, because of which the mind must employ its powers of memory and expectation as well as that of attention. In order, therefore, that the motion may be measured, the mind's attention must unceasingly transform expectation into memory, as what we usually

89

call the future comes through the present to become the past. The necessity imposed on the soul to grasp the world of succession in piecemeal fashion indicates how its life on earth is a real distention if compared with God's eternal life, in which there is no distention of any kind.[135]

Though it is difficult to say how far Gregory has been influenced, directly or indirectly, by Plotinus, and Augustine in turn by Gregory, we can observe that the position of Gregory on time is a natural intermediary between those of Plotinus and Augustine. Gregory transfers time from the Plotinian principle of soul to the soul of man. He accomplishes this, however, not by adopting a psychological point of departure but by employing the universal distention of the created world in such a way that it becomes self-conscious in man. The wide range of his notion of "distention" manifests a flexibility that is worthy of Plotinus or even Plato, and one that is not retained in Augustine's treatment of time. As a result he offers a view of time that unifies in a very effective manner the different aspects of the problem, the physical as well as the psychological, since everywhere there is the distention of the creature, but it is uniquely relevant to the intellectual life of man.

5. The Moral Aspect of Time

Nor, as we have noted, does Gregory neglect the moral problems that are involved for man in a temporal existence. The moral aspect of time always has a place in the Platonic tradition, but not always the same place. Plato, in defining time as the image of eternity, employs it as a means of assimilating becoming to being, and it therefore has in the dialectic of the *Timaeus* an upward tendency. Plotinus, however, does not follow all the Platonic implications contained in the metaphor of the image, emphasizing rather the differences between eternity and time. By adopting a new method of his own, which in part brings together Platonic statements that are made in different places, he connects the descent of the soul closely with his derivation of time from eternity, and time too is affected by the moral consequences of this procedure. But, even apart from this, one of his favorite dialectical devices is to contrast a higher and a lower stage in his hierarchy by applying to them various pairs of contraries. Both Gregory and Augustine employ the notion of descent to describe the position of the soul in the sensible universe. But there is this important difference between them and Plotinus, namely, that for him the existence of the lower is always implied in that of the higher; but for them the existence of the soul is not necessitated by the existence of God, since both the Christians insist that the universe and man have been created through a free choice of God's will and did not have to come into existence. Yet in both Gregory and Augustine there is a Plotinian insistence that the soul of man collect itself from the dispersion of its existence in a universe of flux, and in this way begin the ascent to eternal life.

As with Gregory, the conception of time as a psychological "distention" leads Augustine very readily to think of it as a distention or distraction in the moral sense. The soul not only adapts itself to a world in which reality is presented to it in succession, but it also finds a diversity of interests that distract it from its real purpose for existing. The relation between time as a psychological distention and as a moral distraction is well brought out by a sentence from the *Confessions* (11. 29. 39): ". . . You, Lord, are my eternal Father; but I have fallen apart into times, whose order I do not know, and by turbulent vicissitudes my thoughts are torn asunder, the inmost entrails of my soul, until the time I shall flow into You, purified and molten by the fire of Your love." To Plotinus the conception of the soul collecting itself from the dispersion of the temporal existence into which it has fallen would not seem strange, nor would it to Gregory, who would also understand, as Plotinus could not easily do, the function of the divine love. But with Augustine it is not a question of looking at the world and the position of man in it from the outside, as it were. He has felt the distraction, the tearing apart of his own soul, and he is too well aware that by merely knowing what the goal is and willing to go there he can fail to make the journey. His words tell the story of a will that became effective only after long struggle and with providential help from outside itself.

Thus the notion of time as a distracting and disruptive force in human life is related within Augustine's own soul to his psychological analysis of time itself, which tells him that it is a distention of his mind by which he measures the succession around him. In arriving at this view he is very much indebted to those who took up the problem before him, and the elements he employs can as a whole be found elsewhere as well. If we examine the treatment of time that most closely resembles his among his predecessors, that of Gregory, it is clear that Augustine has gone beyond this in the explicitness of detail he gives to the mental activities of memory and expectation, which Gregory, by a stroke that might even be called revolutionary, came to employ as equivalents of past and future. But Augustine does not merely amplify such a doctrine as that of Gregory by continuing along lines already laid down. He takes an entirely new starting point, not looking at the way in which a universal distention might be found relevant to man, but examining the operation of time within his own mind. Only later does he employ such a traditional term as "distention" to articulate the findings he has made by this new mode of philosophical analysis, and the term now takes on a new meaning in conformity with the introspective framework the philosopher has constructed.

6. Conclusion

Augustine, like any great thinker, has devised a new method of acquiring knowledge, and it is not limited to a single area. His view that time is a distention—and a distraction—of the mind, arrived at by starting from his thoughts of time and of temporal phenomena, is paralleled by his interpretation of the soul's flight to God in terms of his own internal struggles of intellect and will to make that flight, and likewise by the version of the ontological argument for God's existence that he formulates from the idea of God that sustains him in the depths of his immersion in the problem of evil. Everywhere there is the beginning within, and everywhere the thought bears the marks of the whole man.

We have been examining, in these three instances, not merely a series of historical and philosophical influences, but the continuation and perpetual renovation of one of the basic methods by which man may seek the truth. This method, taken in the larger sense, has its origins in the earliest philosophy of the western world, and by the time that Greek philosophy has to a large extent been fused with the scriptural heritage of Christianity the method has arrived at an advanced stage of flexibility and sophistication. It is at this point that Augustine appears on the scene, with the theoretical groundwork already well laid for him. Through the force of his peculiar genius he was able to take the doctrines he had received and refashion them with his mind and with his heart. Doctrines that had tended, if truth be told, to become formulas, applied too automatically and oftentimes indiscriminately, took on a new life when they entered the soul of this man who was himself so conscious of what was going on in the life of his soul. He carried further the anthropocentric tendency of Greek Christian thought to make his own philosophy, one might say, Augustinocentric. Yet in so doing he not only infused new concreteness and vitality into this tradition, but he also gave it a more universal validity and a wider appeal. If philosophy, which with good reason might be called a Greek way of looking at things,[136] has been able to span the gap of the centuries to the Middle Ages and to our own world, it has found no stronger support or one more deeply needed at a given time than it has in Augustine.

Notes

1. *Prosl.*, Prooem., . . . considerans illud esse multorum concatenatione contextum argumentorum, coepi mecum quaerere, si forte posset inveniri unum argumentum, quod nullo alio ad se probandum quam se solo indigeret, et solum ad astruendum quia deus vere est, et quia est summum bonum nullo alio indigens, et quo omnia indigent ut sint et ut bene sint, et quaecumque de divina credimus substantia, sufficeret.

2. *Ibid.*, ch. 2, . . . Et quidem credimus te esse aliquid quo nihil maius cogitari possit. . . . Et certe id quo maius cogitari nequit, non potest esse in solo intellectu. Si enim vel in solo intellectu est, potest cogitari esse et in re, quod maius est. Si ergo id quo maius cogitari non potest, est in solo intellectu: id ipsum quo maius cogitari non potest, est quo maius cogitari potest. Sed certe hoc esse non potest. Existit ergo procul dubio aliquid quo maius cogitari non valet, et in intellectu et in re.

3. *De doct. christ.* 1. 7. 7, Nam cum ille unus cogitatur deorum Deus, ab his etiam qui alios et suspicantur et vocant et colunt deos sive in coelo sive in terra, ita cogitatur, ut aliquid quo nihil melius sit atque sublimius illa cogitatio conetur attingere. Speaking of this passage Étienne Gilson, *Introduction à l'étude de saint Augustin*[3] (Paris, 1949), p. 218, n. 2, says, "Cette formule est une des sources probables de saint Anselme, *Proslogion,* cap. II." The relation between this passage and Anselm's thought is discussed at length by Th.-André Audet, "Une source augustinienne de l'argument de saint Anselme," in J. Maritain, *Étienne Gilson, philosophe de la chrétienté* (*Rencontres,* XXX [Paris, 1949]), pp. 105–142.

4. See also *De doct. christ.* 1. 7. 7, Omnes tamen certatim pro excellentia Dei dimicant; nec quisquam inveniri potest qui hoc Deum credat esse quo melius aliquid

est. Itaque hoc omnes Deum consentiunt esse, quod ceteris rebus omnibus anteponunt.

5. *Conf.* 7. 4. 6, Sic enim nitebar invenire cetera, ut iam inveneram melius esse incorruptibile quam corruptibile, et ideo te, quidquid esses, esse incorruptibilem confitebar. Neque enim ulla anima umquam potuit poteritve cogitare aliquid, quod sit te melius, qui summum et optimum bonum es. Cum autem verissime atque certissime incorruptibile corruptibili praeponatur, sicut iam ego praeponebam, poteram iam cogitatione aliquid adtingere, quod esset melius deo meo, nisi tu esses incorruptibilis. Note the words *potuit poteritve cogitare,* reflected in Anselm's various expressions such as *cogitari possit* (see n. 2), but not to be found in the passage from *De doct. christ.* (see n. 3).

The similarity of this passage from the *Conf.* to the argument of Anselm's *Prosl.* was noted and briefly commented on by J. Draeseke, "Sur la question des sources d'Anselme," *Revue de philosophie,* XV (1909), 650–653. He says, p. 652, "Anselme n'avait-il pas dû se reporter instinctivement à ce passage où Augustin reprend une fois de plus son idée fondamentale sur l'être divin, l'approfondit, la développe, et cela déjà, même quant à la forme, de la façon qui chez Anselme est si frappante, à savoir par l'emploi répété de l'ablatif de comparaison, qu'on trouve aussi chez Boèce?" Following Draeseke, Émile Bréhier, *Histoire de la philosophie,* I (Paris, 1928), 561, says, "Le mouvement de pensée est le même: on peut sûrement attribuer à Dieu ce qu'on ne peut en nier sans diminuer sa perfection. . . . Mais nulle part, on n'avait songé à faire de l'existence un attribut qu'on ne peut lui refuser en raison de sa grandeur et de l'immensité de sa perfection." J. Gibb and W. Montgomery, *The Confessions of Augustine* (Cambridge, 1927), p. 171, state, "The argument is closely parallel in form to Anselm's famous 'proof,' in the *Proslogium,* of God's existence."

There is a striking similarity to Augustine (noted by

Draeseke, above) in Boethius, *De consol. philos.* 3. 10,
Deum rerum omnium principem bonum esse communis
humanorum conceptio probat animorum. Nam cum nihil
deo melius excogitari queat, id quo melius nihil est
bonum esse quis dubitet? Ita vero bonum esse deum
ratio demonstrat, ut perfectum quoque in eo bonum esse
convincat. Nam ni tale sit, rerum omnium princeps esse
non poterit. Erit enim eo praestantius aliquid perfectum
possidens bonum, quod hoc prius atque antiquius esse
videatur. . . . Quare quod a summo bono diversum est
sui natura, id summum bonum non est—quod nefas est de
eo cogitare quo nihil constat esse praestantius. Here
a number of features of Augustine's argument are
to be found, even though they have been adapted by
Boethius to a different line of argumentation. A certain
likeness of terminology may be observed as far back as
Seneca, *Natur. quaest.* 1, Praef. 13, quid est deus? mens
universi. . . . quod vides totum et quod non vides totum.
sic demum magnitudo illi sua redditur, qua nihil maius
cogitari potest, si solus est omnia, si opus suum et intra et
extra tenet; perhaps even in Horace, *Carm.* 4. 2. 37–38,
quo nihil maius meliusve terris fata donavere bonique
divi.

6. *Conf.* 7. 4. 6.

7. Frag. 32 (Diels-Kranz[6], from which all citations to
the Pre-Socratics will be taken).

8. E.g., frag. 70 (Sidgwick), Zeus is the ether, Zeus
the earth, and Zeus the sky; Zeus is the universe and
what is still higher than this.

9. *Heracles* 1345–1346. So Parmenides, speaking of his
own discovery, that which is, says that it is not in need
(frag. 8. 33).

10. His use of the word θέμις in this connection (frag.
8. 32), the function of which is comparable to that of
Xenophanes' "fitting," anticipates Plato's more theological employment of the same word (see n. 11). L. Woodbury has some relevant remarks on the interpretation of

frag. 3, "Parmenides on Names," *Harvard Studies in Classical Philology,* LXIII (1958), 156–157.

11. *Tim.* 29A; cf. 30A.

12. Gilson has employed this scriptural passage extensively to elaborate a basic difference between the metaphysics of Greek and that of Christian philosophy, the latter reaching its climax in Thomas Aquinas. He says, e.g., *God and Philosophy* (New Haven, 1946), p. 61, "Like all Christians, but unlike the Greeks, Augustine has a quite clear notion of what it is to create something 'out of nothing.' It is to make it to be. What still remains Greek in Augustine's thought is his very notion of what it is to be. His ontology, or science of being, is an 'essential' rather than an 'existential' one. In other words, it exhibits a marked tendency to reduce the existence of a thing to its essence, and to answer the question: What is it for a thing to be? by saying: It is to be that which it is." It seems to me possible that in this highly illuminating construction there are some generalizations that tend to be exaggerated, with a consequent and not entirely justifiable stress on the "non-existential" character of Greek and early Christian metaphysics. Moreover, I wonder how far, in the development of metaphysics, the formula of Exodus was a source of interpretation rather than a statement that itself required to be interpreted, as was true of so many scriptural statements that received varying philosophical interpretations. I have touched on some aspects of this general problem in "Greek Philosophy and the Cappadocian Cosmology," *Dumbarton Oaks Papers,* XII (Cambridge, Mass., 1958), 29–57.

13. *Contra Eunomium,* ed. Jaeger[2] (Leiden, 1960), II, 251, 1–2 (*P[atrologia] G[raeca],* XLV, 840D). It is interesting to note that Gregory bases his statement here on Hebrews 11. 6, which says that one approaching God must believe that He is.

14. *De anima et resurr., PG,* XLVI, 93B.

15. *Contra Eunomium* (see n. 13), II, 186, 9–14 (*PG, XLV*, 768C–769A). He goes on to say that any view that refers non-being to "Him who really is" (τὸν ὄντως ὄντα) is a denial of true divinity.

16. W. Jaeger, *The Theology of the Early Greek Philosophers* (Oxford, 1947), p. 50, states that through the Stoics this term "came down to the Church Fathers, who made it one of the corner-stones of Christian theology. The postulate of the θεοπρεπές is fundamental to the allegorical interpretation of Homer's tales of the gods in Stoicism."

17. *Contra Eunomium* (see n. 13), I, 287, 4–6 (*PG, XLV*, 981A). Gregory also says here, very much in the manner of Xenophanes (frag. 24), that the divine is all sight and hearing and knowing.

18. *Ibid.*, II, 315, 18–20 (*PG, XLV*, 469C). Another echo of Plato (*Tim.* 29E; *Phaedrus* 247A) is the statement, made by Gregory in the course of his arguments about the Holy Spirit, that envy cannot touch the divine nature, *Adv. Maced.*, ed. Müller (Leiden, 1958), 99. 23 (*PG, XLV*, 1316D).

19. *Ibid.*, 91. 4-8 (*PG, XLV*, 1304D). The context here indicates how closely the God-befitting conception and the proper terminology are related in Gregory's mind to the being of God itself.

20. *Ibid.*, 94. 3–7 (*PG, XLV*, 1309B); *Orat. cat.* 20 (*PG, XLV*, 56D).

21. *Ibid.*, Praef. (*PG, XLV*, 12C). Cf. *Contra Eunomium* (see n. 13), II, 186, 24–26 (*PG, XLV*, 769A); *Adv. Maced.* (see n. 18), 91. 8–12 (*PG, XLV*, 1304D–1305A).

22. *Ibid.*, 91. 4–12 (*PG, XLV*, 1304D–1305A); cf. *ibid.*, 94. 3–19 (*PG, XLV*, 1309A–C). The importance of the name "God" in discussing the three divine persons is stressed in *Ex commun. notion.*, ed. Müller (Leiden, 1958), 19. 1–20. 13 (*PG, XLV*, 176A–C).

23. *Adv. Maced.* (see n. 18), 92. 10–25 (*PG, XLV*, 1305C–D). In this passage, after distinguishing between

"truly" and "just in name," Gregory proceeds to use "name," as he often does, in close connection with, and even standing for, that which is "truly" signified. He also points out that, because the divine nature is simple, it does not possess the various attributes, such as goodness, power, and wisdom, by participation, but it *is* itself each of these.

24. *In inscript. Psalm.*, ed. McDonough (Leiden, 1962), 79. 6–12 (*PG*, XLIV, 500A–B); *De orat. dom.* 3, *PG*, XLIV, 1156B; *Adv. Maced.* (see n. 18), 96. 19–22 (*PG*, XLV, 1312D).

25. *Adv. Arium et Sab.*, ed. Müller (Leiden, 1958), 81. 22–24 (*PG*, XLV, 1296B).

26. *Adv. Apolin.*, ed. Müller (Leiden, 1958), 197. 1–2 (*PG*, XLV, 1216C).

27. *Adv. Maced.* (see n. 18), 105. 16–18 (*PG*, XLV, 1324D). (On the absence of need, cf. n. 9.)

28. *Sum. theol.*, I, qu. 2, art. 1, ad 2um, . . . forte ille qui audit hoc nomen, Deus, non intelligit significari aliquid quo maius cogitari non possit, cum quidam crediderint Deum esse corpus. Dato etiam quod quilibet intelligat hoc nomine, Deus, significari hoc quod dicitur (scilicet illud quo maius cogitari non potest), non tamen propter hoc sequitur quod intelligat id quod significatur per nomen esse in rerum natura, sed in apprehensione intellectus tantum. Nec potest argui quod sit in re, nisi daretur quod sit in re aliquid quo maius cogitari non potest; quod non est datum a ponentibus Deum non esse.

29. E.g., *In Eccles.*, ed. Alexander (Leiden, 1962), 412. 12–19 (*PG*, XLIV, 729C).

30. *De civ. Dei* 6. 5, . . . in hoc, ut dii furati sint, ut adulterarint, ut servierint homini.

31. *In Iohan. evang.* 13. 5.

32. *Conf.* 1. 4. 4, et vae tacentibus de te, quoniam loquaces muti sunt. A variation on this is found in *In*

Iohan. evang. 13. 5, omnia possunt dici de Deo, et nihil digne dicitur de Deo; this is almost exactly like a passage in Gregory of Nyssa, *De beatitud.* 1, *PG*, XLIV, 1197A–B. For Augustine, cf. *De doct. christ.* 1. 6. 6, Quae pugna verborum silentio cavenda potius quam voce pacanda est. Et tamen Deus, cum de illo nihil digne dici possit, admisit humanae vocis obsequium, et verbis nostris in laude sua gaudere nos voluit. The "time for silence" is discussed by Gregory, *In Eccles.* (see n. 29), 414. 9–15 (*PG*, XLIV, 732A).

33. E.g., *De vera relig.* 55. 113, . . . nisi Deus summe bonus esset, qui et nulli naturae, quae ab ipso bona esse posset, invidit . . .; *ibid.* 13. 26, . . . invidentia, qua diabolus utique diabolus est?

34. *Conf.* 1. 4. 4, zelas et securus es.

35. *De lib. arbit.* 2. 2. 5.

36. *De div. quaest. LXXXIII* 46. 2.

37. *De trin.* 7. 5. 10. Cf. *In Iohan. evang.* 39. 8, Deus autem hoc est quod est; ideo proprium nomen sibi tenuit: Ego sum qui sum. V. J. Bourke has some very perceptive remarks on Augustine's understanding of being, *Augustine's View of Reality* (Villanova, 1964), pp. 7–18. (Cf. n. 12 above.)

38. E.g., Gregory of Nyssa, *Contra Eunomium* (see n. 13), II, 253, 12–13 (*PG*, XLV, 844A). In addition, there are those who state that nothing may be more properly understood of God than that He is. So Hilary, *De trin.* 1. 5, non enim aliud proprium magis Deo quam esse intellegitur. This anticipates the statement of Thomas Aquinas, *Sum. theol.*, I, qu. 13, art. 11, *Sed contra,* Ergo hoc nomen, qui est, est maxime proprium nomen Dei. There is a typical variation in Ambrose, *Explan. Psalm. XII* 43. 20 (Petschenig), nihil tam proprium dei quam semper esse.

39. *Conf.* 4. 16. 28–29.

40. *In Iohan. evang.* 1. 8. Cf. *De doct. christ.* 1. 6. 6, and the remarks of Audet, *op. cit.* (in n. 3), pp. 109–110.

41. See, e.g., the passage of Aquinas quoted in n. 38. The importance of Gregory of Nyssa in the tradition regarding the names of Christ is discussed by W. Jaeger, "Die asketisch-mystische Theologie des Gregor von Nyssa," *Humanistische Reden und Vorträge*[2] (Berlin, 1960), p. 276.

42. *Conf.* 7. 1. 1. Some of the same ideas are expressed in *De doct. christ.* 1. 8. 8.

43. The question of Ambrose's influence on Augustine in another connection will arise at a later point. See, e.g., the reference in n. 84.

44. *Conf.* 7. 2. 3.

45. *Conf.* 7. 3. 4–5.

46. *Tim.* 29E–30A; *Rep.* 509B.

47. *Tim.* 30A.

48. *Tim.* 48A.

49. *De mot. an.* 699b32–700a3. Cf. *Iliad* 8. 17–27.

50. *Metaph.* 1072b3.

51. *Enn.* 6. 8. 20–21.

52. Frag. 1. 26–28.

53. Frag. 2. 6; 8. 17.

54. *Phaedo* 98B–C; *Metaph.* 985a18–21 (but, for a more favorable judgment, cf. 984b15–22).

55. Frag. 12.

56. *Rep.* 509B.

57. E.g., *Enn.* 6. 7. 23; 6. 9. 6.

58. *Enn.* 3. 8. 9.

59. *Enn.* 6. 9. 5.

60. Gilson, *The Unity of Philosophical Experience* (New York, 1947), pp. 106–108, has some interesting remarks on philosophical influence. He says, e.g., "The recurrence of certain philosophical attitudes is an historical fact. It cannot be explained away merely by resorting to the influence of a philosopher on another philosopher."

61. In the passive we may have an echo of the *De doct. christ.* (see n. 3).

62. Also found *ibid.* (see nn. 3 and 4).

63. *Prosl.*, ch. 3, Quod utique sic vere est, ut nec cogitari possit non esse. Nam potest cogitari esse aliquid, quod non possit cogitari non esse; quod maius est quam quod non esse cogitari potest. Quare si id quo maius nequit cogitari, potest cogitari non esse: id ipsum quo maius cogitari nequit, non est id quo maius cogitari nequit; quod convenire non potest. Sic ergo vere est aliquid quo maius cogitari non potest, ut nec cogitari possit non esse. Et hoc es tu, domine deus noster. Sic ergo vere es, domine deus meus, ut nec cogitari possis non esse. Et merito. Si enim aliqua mens posset cogitare aliquid melius te, ascenderet creatura super creatorem, et iudicaret de creatore; quod valde est absurdum.

64. A phrase similar to *cogitatione adtingere* is used in the *De doct. christ.* (see n. 3).

65. *Prosl.*, Prooem.

66. *Monol.*, Prolog., Quam ego saepe retractans nihil potui invenire me in ea dixisse, quod non catholicorum patrum et maxime beati Augustini scriptis cohaereat. It should be noted that there is an important variant reading that may represent a *prior recensio* of Anselm himself: in catholicorum patrum et maxime beati Augustini scriptis inveniatur aut illis cohaereat. In *S. Anselmi Cant. Arch. opera omnia,* recens. F. S. Schmitt (Edinburgh, 1946), I, cf. the critical apparatus for the passage, p. 8, and the *Praemonenda* of the editor, p. 4.

67. This is discussed in detail by H. Merki, Ὁμοίωσις Θεῷ, *von der platonischen Angleichung an Gott zur Gott-ähnlichkeit bei Gregor von Nyssa* (Freiburg in der Schweiz, 1952).

68. See n. 38.

69. *Sum. theol.,* I, qu. 2, art. 3, *Resp.*

70. See n. 1.

71. This is clearly not the meaning of "ontological" in the Wolffian sense, which is the one, historically speaking, that is pertinent to the origin of the name. See Gilson, *Being and Some Philosophers* (Toronto, 1949), pp. 119–

121. Cf. the remarks along a somewhat different line in his *L'esprit de la philosophie médiévale²* (Paris, 1944), pp. 58–62.

72. *Quid ad haec respondeat quidam pro insipiente,* recens. Schmitt (see n. 66), ch. 6.

73. *Op. cit.* (in n. 3), p. 26, "C'est pourquoi, de même qu'elle prépare sous son premier aspect le symbolisme médiéval du monde sensible, envisagée sous ce deuxième aspect, elle ouvre la voie aux spéculations métaphysiques d'un saint Anselme, qui cherchent à découvrir l'existence de Dieu dans l'idée même que nous avons de lui. Non qu'il ait développé cette preuve, mais saint Augustin n'en avait pas moins certainement engagé la recherche dans une direction qui conduisait normalement à la preuve du *Proslogion.*"

74. "Sens et nature de l'argument de saint Anselme," *Archives d'histoire doctrinale et littéraire du moyen âge,* IX (1934), 15. This view is disputed by Audet, *op. cit.* (in n. 3), p. 121.

75. Sextus Empiricus, *Phys.* 1. 20–22; Aristotle, frag. 10 (Rose, 1886). Something similar is stated by Plato, *Laws* 966D–E.

A somewhat different approach to this entire problem may be found in R. M. Jones, "Posidonius and the Flight of the Mind," *Classical Philology,* XXI (1926), 97–113.

76. Many of the doctrines of the Orphics are a matter of dispute, and they probably always will be. But current differences of opinion on this subject are not directly relevant to us here. Generally moderate accounts may be found in Jaeger, *op. cit.* (in n. 16), pp. 83–89, and in E. R. Dodds, *The Greeks and the Irrational* (Berkeley and Los Angeles, 1951), pp. 135–156. See also Jaeger, "The Greek Ideas of Immortality," *op. cit.* (in n. 41), pp. 291–296.

77. Frag. 131 (Schroeder). Xenophon, *Cyr.* 8. 7. 21, says that it is during sleep that the soul appears most divine.

78. Frag. 115. 13.

79. Socrates manifests a certain caution in speaking of the after-life also at *Apol.* 29A–B, 40C. It is very difficult to refer such an attitude to Socrates rather than to Plato, as, e.g., Jaeger attempts to do, "The Greek Ideas of Immortality," *op. cit.* (in n. 41), p. 294.

80. Cf. *Gorg.* 493C, where Socrates indicates that a fable, absurd though it may be, can have a moral purpose.

81. This is in contrast to the kind of seeing mentioned by Plotinus as relevant to beauty in the opening sentence of the treatise.

82. Paul Henry, S.J., *Saint Augustine on Personality* (New York, 1960).

83. *Plotin et l'Occident* (Louvain, 1934), pp. 104–116. Augustine writes, *Conf.* 8. 8. 19, et non illuc ibatur navibus aut quadrigis aut pedibus, quantum saltem de domo in eum locum ieram, ubi sedebamus. nam non solum ire verum etiam pervenire illuc nihil erat aliud quam velle ire, sed velle fortiter et integre, non semisauciam hac atque hac versare et iactare voluntatem parte adsurgente cum alia parte cadente luctantem. In Augustine's terminology here there is a possible echo of Horace, *Epist.* 1. 11. 28–29, navibus atque quadrigis petimus bene vivere.

84. Pierre Courcelle, *Recherches sur les Confessions de saint Augustin* (Paris, 1950), pp. 124–132. Augustine states, *Conf.* 1. 18. 28, nam longe a vultu tuo in affectu tenebroso. non enim pedibus aut spatiis locorum itur abs te aut reditur ad te, aut vero filius ille tuus minor equos vel currus vel naves quaesivit aut avolavit pinna visibili aut moto poplite iter egit, ut in longinqua regione vivens prodige dissiparet quod dederas proficiscenti dulcis pater, quia dederas, et egeno redeunti dulcior: in affectu ergo libidinoso, id enim est tenebroso atque id est longe a vultu tuo.

There is also the controversial question, which cannot be taken up here, of the extent to which Augustine was familiar with the doctrines of Neo-Platonism through Porphyry. An important recent contribution on this subject, with references to some of the literature, is H. Dörrie, "Das fünffach gestufte Mysterium. Der Aufstieg der Seele bei Porphyrios und Ambrosius," *Mullus* (Münster, 1964), pp. 79–92. He states, e.g., p. 86, "Der THEILER'sche Arbeitssatz ist nicht nur für Augustin . . . gültig. Nicht Plotin . . . sondern Porphyrios ist der Vater des Neuplatonismus in lateinischer Sprache." Interesting parallels for the flight of the soul may be found in W. Theiler, "Antike und christliche Rückkehr zu Gott," *ibid.*, pp. 352–361.

85. Plotinus requires that the inner eye be strong and vigorous by its purity, *Enn.* 1. 6. 9; cf. 6. 9. 9.

86. *De Isaac vel anima* 8. 78–79 (Schenkl), the most interesting section of which is as follows: fugiamus ergo in patriam verissimam [Courcelle wonders if *carissimam* is to be read here for Plotinus' φίλην, *Enn.* 1. 6. 8 (as indeed Augustine employs it for the same purpose, *De civ. Dei* 9. 17); Plotinus uses ἀληθέστερον in this same sentence, and a little earlier he has used ἀληθινόν]. illic patria nobis et illic pater, a quo creati sumus, ubi est Hierusalem civitas, quae est mater omnium [cf. Galat. 4. 26]. sed quae est fuga? non utique pedum, qui sunt corporis; isti enim quocumque currunt in terra currunt et de solo ad solum transeunt. nec navibus fugiamus aut curribus aut equis, qui obligantur et cadunt [cf. Ps. 19. 8–9], sed fugiamus animo et oculis aut pedibus interioribus. Courcelle discusses this passage in "Plotin et saint Ambroise," *Revue de philologie,* XXIV (1950), 36–37.

87. The return of Odysseus is a symbol for Plotinus of the ascent of the soul, as, e.g., in the allusion at *Enn.* 5. 9. 1. Cf. Courcelle, "Quelques symboles funéraires du néo-platonisme latin: Le vol de Dédale.—Ulysse et les Sirènes," *Revue des études anciennes,* XLVI (1944), 75–76. For Odysseus as a model for the intellectual journey of Parmenides see E. A. Havelock, "Parmenides and

Odysseus," *Harvard Studies in Classical Philology*, LXIII (1958), 133–143.

88. *De orat. dom.* 2, *PG*, XLIV, 1144B–1145C, the most important part of which, for our purposes, is the following (words of greater interest are spaced; for the text see Preface):

ὥσπερ τοίνυν ἐκεῖ τῆς παρὰ τοῦ πατρὸς φιλανθρωπίας αἰτία γέγονε τῷ νέῳ ἡ πρὸς τὴν πατρῴαν ἑστίαν ἐπιστροφή—αὕτη δὲ ἦν ὁ οὐρανὸς εἰς ὃν πεπλημμεληκέναι τῷ πατρὶ λέγει—οὕτω καὶ ἐνταῦθα δοκεῖ μοι διδάσκων ὁ κύριος τὸν ἐν τοῖς οὐρανοῖς ἐπικαλεῖσθαι πατέρα μνήμην σοι ποιεῖν τῆς ἀ γ α θ ῆ ς π α τ ρ ί δ ο ς, ὡς ἂν ἐπιθυμίαν σφοδροτέραν τῶν καλῶν ἐμποιήσας ἐπιστήσειέ σε τ ῇ ὁ δ ῷ τ ῇ π ρ ὸ ς τ ὴ ν π α τ ρ ί δ α π ά λ ι ν ἐ π α ν α γ ο ύ σ ῃ. ὁδὸς δὲ ἡ πρὸς τὸν οὐρανὸν τὴν ἀνθρωπίνην φύσιν ἀνάγουσα ο ὐ δ ε μ ί α τ ί ς ἐ σ τ ι ν ἄ λ λ η ε ἰ μ ὴ φυγὴ καὶ ἀπόστασις τῶν περιγείων κακῶν· τῆς δὲ φυγῆς τῶν κακῶν ἡ ἐπίνοια ο ὐ κ ἄ λ λ η μ ο ί τ ι ς ε ἶ ν α ι δ ο κ ε ῖ π λ ὴ ν τ ῆ ς π ρ ὸ ς τ ὸ ν θ ε ὸ ν ὁ μ ο ι ώ σ ε ω ς. τὸ δὲ ὁμοιωθῆναι θεῷ τὸ δίκαιόν τε καὶ ὅσιον καὶ ἀγαθὸν καὶ τὰ τοιαῦτά ἐστι γενέσθαι. ὧν εἴ τις τοὺς χαρακτῆρας, ὡς ἔστι δυνατόν, ἐναργῶς ἐν ἑαυτῷ τυπώσειεν, ἀ μ ο γ η τ ὶ κ α τ ὰ τ ὸ α ὐ τ ό μ α τ ο ν πρὸς τὸν οὐράνιον χῶρον ἀπὸ τοῦ περιγείου μεταναστήσεται βίου. οὐ γὰρ τ ο π ι κ ὴ τοῦ θείου πρὸς τὸ ἀνθρώπινόν ἐστιν ἡ δ ι ά σ τ α σ ι ς ὥστε τινὸς μ η χ α ν ῆ ς ἡμῖν καὶ ἐπινοίας γενέσθαι χρείαν τὸ βαρύ τε καὶ ἐμβριθὲς καὶ γεῶδες τοῦτο σαρκίον πρὸς τὴν ἀσώματόν τε καὶ νοερὰν διαγωγὴν μετοικίζειν· ἀλλὰ νοητῶς τῆς ἀρετῆς τοῦ κακοῦ κεχωρισμένης ἐν μόνῃ τῇ π ρ ο α ι ρ έ σ ε ι τοῦ ἀνθρώπου κεῖται πρὸς ὅπερ ἂν ἐπικλιθείη τῇ ἐπιθυμίᾳ ἐν ἐκείνῳ εἶναι. ἐπεὶ οὖν οὐδεὶς ἔπεστι πόνος ἑλέσθαι τὸ ἀγαθόν, τῷ δὲ ἑλέσθαι καὶ τὸ τυχεῖν ἔπεται ὧν τις προείλετο, ἔ ξ ε σ τ ί σοι εὐθὺς ἐν τῷ οὐρανῷ εἶναι τὸν θεὸν ἐν τῇ διανοίᾳ λαβόντι. εἰ γάρ, καθώς φησιν ὁ Ἐκκλησιαστής, Ὁ θεὸς ἐν τῷ οὐρανῷ, σὺ δὲ τῷ θεῷ, κατὰ τὸν προφήτην, προσεκολλήθης, ἀνάγκη πᾶσα τὸν τῷ θεῷ συνημμένον ἐκεῖ εἶναι ὅπου ἐστὶν ὁ θεός. προστάξας τοίνυν ἐν τῇ προσευχῇ λέγειν πατέρα ἑαυτοῦ τὸν θεόν, ο ὐ δ ὲ ν ἕ τ ε ρ ο ν ἢ ὁμοιοῦσθαί σε τῇ θ ε ο π ρ ε π ε ῖ πολιτείᾳ τῷ οὐρανίῳ κελεύει πατρί, καθάπερ καὶ φανερώτερον ἑτέρωθι τὸ τοιοῦτον παρεγγυᾷ λέγων, Γίνεσθε τέλειοι καθὼς καὶ ὁ πατὴρ ὑμῶν τέλειός ἐστιν.

89. Plotinus uses in this connection the words ἀγών and

108

πόνος, *Enn.* 1. 6. 7. For Gregory, in whom the idea is very important, virtue is acquired only by much sweat and toil, e.g., *De beatitud.* 6, *PG,* XLIV, 1273B. Its role in the asceticism of Gregory is discussed by Jaeger, *op. cit.* (in n. 41), pp. 267, 279. For the flight of the soul in Gregory see also J. Daniélou, *Platonisme et théologie mystique* (Paris, 1944), pp. 38–49.

90. *Op. cit.* (in n. 83), p. 110.

91. Here too he corrects himself, saying, *Retract.* 1. 4. 3, that he had not meant to subscribe to the doctrine of Porphyry that we should flee from all that is body.

92. In speaking of the prodigal son, *Conf.* 1. 18. 28, Augustine includes flying of a physical kind (*avolavit pinna visibili*) in the modes of transportation that cannot be employed. This is an addition to the list of Plotinus, *Enn.* 1. 6. 8. It is interesting to note that Augustine, *Conf.* 8. 8. 19, speaking of the proper means of travel, uses the word *integer* again (*velle fortiter et integre*). His *voluntas* is now seen to be the invisible wing that must be whole. Augustine's use of flying in this connection is discussed by Courcelle, *op. cit.* (in n. 87), pp. 68–69, including a reference to Daedalus in which there seems to be an echo of Plotinus (1. 6. 8), *Contra Acad.* 3. 2. 3, Nam ut sine navi, vel quolibet vehiculo, aut omnino, ne vel ipsum Daedalum timeam, sine ullis ad hanc rem accommodatis instrumentis, aut aliqua occultiore potentia, Aegeum mare nemo transmittit, quamvis nihil aliud, quam pervenire proponat, quod cum ei evenerit, illa omnia quibus advectus est, paratus sit abjicere atque contemnere: ita quisquis ad sapientiae portum . . .; cf. *ibid.* 3. 2. 4, . . . quo ad sapientiam pervehamur.

93. We find the metaphor of the eye in this work also, *Contra Acad.* 2. 3. 7, Ergo ille, si veram pulchritudinem cujus falsae amator est, sanatis renudatisque paululum oculis posset intueri, quanta voluptate philosophiae gremio se involveret?

94. There is considerable controversy as to the extent to which Augustine admits a fall of the soul into the body and in what sense he means this, a complex question that cannot be taken up here. For a careful study of the chief texts of Augustine and their relation to Plotinus see R. J. O'Connell, S.J., "The Plotinian Fall of the Soul in St. Augustine," *Traditio,* XIX (1963), 1–35.

95. The Plotinian background in *Enn.* 1. 6. 8 of this passage as a whole is clear. The men who are kept from their fatherland by contrary winds may represent Odysseus, while the activities of walking and sailing, instead of being denied, as in Plotinus and Augustine himself elsewhere (*Conf.* 1. 18. 28; 8. 8. 19), are reinterpreted in a positive way and with a moral coloring that is added to the Plotinian notion of seeing.

Cf. *De doct. christ.* 1. 4. 4; 1. 11. 11–12. 12. In 1. 39. 43 Augustine stresses the importance of charity; the man who has faith, hope, and charity needs Scripture only for the instruction of others. (Is this an echo of Plotinus' dispensing with a guide, 1. 6. 9, just as the subsequent use of *machinis* recalls the previous chapter of Plotinus?)

96. E.g., *Enn.* 5. 1. 1; 6. 9. 9. (The latter describes a prodigal daughter.)

97. *Op. cit.* (in n. 84), pp. 126–127.

98. This passage is discussed by Henry, *op. cit.* (in n. 83), pp. 110–111.

99. See n. 102 for a similar expression in *De civ. Dei.* The type is by no means unusual in Augustine.

100. E.g., *Conf.* 3. 4. 7, surgere coeperam, ut ad te redirem; 4. 16. 30, itaque mihi non ad usum, sed ad perniciem magis valebat, quia tam bonam partem substantiae meae sategi habere in potestate et fortitudinem meam non ad te custodiebam [cf. Ps. 58. 10], sed profectus sum abs te in longinquam regionem, ut eam dissiparem in meretrices cupiditates. The association of ideas is especially interesting in the latter passage, where Augustine utilizes the scriptural texts to explain his own

situation and at the same time interweaves reminiscences of the Plotinian descent of the soul, as set forth, e.g., in *Enn.* 3. 7. 11, where the creative principle is said to be desirous of being master of itself and thus to dissipate its inner unity in a world of multiplicity, weakening itself in the process. The basic importance of the prodigal son as a theme of the *Conf.* as a whole is stressed by O'Connell, "The Riddle of Augustine's 'Confessions': A Plotinian Key," *International Philosophical Quarterly,* IV (1964), 327–372.

101. *Op. cit.* (in n. 84), p. 128.

102. This passage (*De civ. Dei* 9. 17) also contains an expression like the *nihil erat aliud quam* of *Conf.* 8. 8. 19 already discussed: nulla est ab illo alia longinquitas quam eius dissimilitudo. The two contexts are related in that the *longinquitas,* if it consists in nothing else than *dissimilitudo,* requires, not any physical means of transport, but nothing else than the will to go towards God.

103. *Op. cit.* (in n. 84), pp. 110–117, 120–122.

104. *Op. cit.* (in n. 83), p. 110. He also discusses this point in Plotinus, *The Enneads* (New York, 1957), Introd., p. 1.

105. See, e.g., L. Bogliolo's article, "Significato e attualità dell' interiorità agostiniana," *S. Agostino e le grandi correnti della filosofia contemporanea* (Rome, 1956), pp. 319–326.

106. *Tim.* 37D. It should be noted that time is included among the works of reason in the dialogue, while space is not.

107. *Phys.* 219b2–3.

108. *Phys.* 223a21–29.

109. A certain psychological interest in time is shown in *De mem. et remin.* 449b25–30; *De sens.* 448a24–30. That the psychological significance of time was not lost on Epicurus is indicated by Diogenes Laertius, *Vita Epicuri* 137.

110. The possibility of a psychological point of view is hinted at in *Enn.* 6. 1. 5. The relation of time and memory is briefly discussed in 4. 4. 8, and some psychological implications of time are set forth in 1. 5.

111. *Enn.* 3. 7. 11–13. I have discussed this passage and its relation to the accounts of Plato and Aristotle in *Four Views of Time in Ancient Philosophy* (Cambridge, Mass., 1948), pp. 118–148. See also G. H. Clark, "The Theory of Time in Plotinus," *The Philosophical Review,* LIII (1944), 337–358.

112. *Enn.* 4. 4. 16.

113. *Contra Eunomium* (see n. 13), I, 136, 8–13 (*PG,* XLV, 365D–368A). Cf. *In Eccles.* (see n. 29), 440. 2–9 (*PG,* XLIV, 752D). Plotinus, *Enn.* 4. 4. 16, had also correlated time and place by saying that sensible things cannot be in the same time any more than in the same place.

114. *In Eccles.* (see n. 29), 376. 23–377. 17 (*PG,* XLIV, 700B–D).

115. *Contra Eunomium* (see n. 13), I, 136, 8–27 (*PG,* XLV, 365D–368B).

116. *In Eccles.* (see n. 29), 437. 21–438. 7 (*PG,* XLIV, 752A); cf. Ecclesiastes 3. 10.

117. *De anima et resurr., PG,* XLVI, 93B.

118. *Hexaemeron, PG,* XXIX, 16C; cf. 12B–C. I have discussed the anthropocentric orientation of the cosmologies of Basil and Gregory, *op. cit.* (in n. 12), with reference, pp. 36–39, 55–57, to this aspect of their treatment of time.

119. I have set forth in greater detail Gregory's theory of time in "Gregory of Nyssa and the Psychological View of Time," *Proceedings of the XIIth International Congress of Philosophy,* XI (Florence, 1960), 59–66. The question is taken up also by Hans von Balthasar, *Présence et pensée, essai sur la philosophie religieuse de Grégoire de Nysse* (Paris, 1942), pp. 2–10.

120. *Conf.* 11. 14. 17.

121. *Phys.* 217b30–218a8.

122. *Phys.* 2. 192.

123. *Phys.* 2. 182–184.

124. *Phys.* 2. 191.

125. *Phys.* 2. 176.

126. *Phys.* 2. 64. Sextus, *Gramm.* 129, uses the same term with reference to the length of syllables, anticipating this "rhetorical" aspect of Augustine's treatment of time, e.g., *Conf.* 11. 26. 33.

127. The dialectical discussion of introspection, *Phys.* 218b21–219a1, along with the reference to the mind (see n. 108), can lead to an exaggeration of the role of the mind in Aristotle's treatment of time, as in W. Bröcker, *Aristoteles* (Frankfurt a. M., 1935), p. 93, a position that I have discussed, *op. cit.* (in n. 111), pp. 45–47.

128. Aristotle has taken up this point, *De mem. et remin.* 450b11–18.

129. *Conf.* 11. 14. 17–22. 28. Note especially 11. 20. 26, Quod autem nunc liquet et claret, nec futura sunt nec praeterita, nec proprie dicitur: tempora sunt tria, praeteritum, praesens et futurum, sed fortasse proprie diceretur: tempora sunt tria, praesens de praeteritis, praesens de praesentibus, praesens de futuris. sunt enim haec in anima tria quaedam et alibi ea non video, praesens de praeteritis memoria, praesens de praesentibus contuitus, praesens de futuris expectatio.

130. *Conf.* 11. 23. 29–30. Note especially 11. 23. 30, nemo ergo mihi dicat caelestium corporum motus esse tempora, quia et cuiusdam voto cum sol stetisset, ut victoriosum proelium perageret, sol stabat, sed tempus ibat. per suum quippe spatium temporis, quod ei sufficeret, illa pugna gesta atque finita est. video igitur tempus quandam esse distentionem.

131. *Adv. Eunomium, PG,* XXIX, 557C–560C. I have taken up the use that Augustine has made of this passage of Basil in "Basil of Caesarea, a New Source for St.

Augustine's Theory of Time," *Harvard Studies in Classical Philology,* LXIII (1958), 437–454. A comparison of Augustine and Basil on this point is especially interesting for the light it throws on Augustine's employment of his sources, in this case an unusually long continuous passage, for his own purposes.

132. Aristotle too, *Phys.* 219a1–3, has come to the same conclusion but in a different way, employing means that are in part psychological, though his view of time is basically physical. Augustine, on the other hand, though his treatment is fundamentally psychological, here attaches time to motion through evidence that is physical and indeed Aristotelian, arriving thereby at a way out of the difficulties his psychological approach has raised.

133. *Conf.* 11. 24. 31–28. 38. Note especially 11. 26. 33, inde mihi visum est nihil esse aliud tempus quam distentionem: sed cuius rei, nescio, et mirum, si non ipsius animi; and 11. 28. 37, Sed quomodo minuitur aut consumitur futurum, quod nondum est, aut quomodo crescit praeteritum, quod iam non est, nisi quia in animo, qui illud agit, tria sunt? nam et expectat et adtendit et meminit, ut id quod expectat per id quod adtendit transeat in id quod meminerit. quis igitur negat futura nondum esse? sed tamen iam est in animo expectatio futurorum. et quis negat praeterita iam non esse? sed tamen adhuc est in animo memoria praeteritorum. et quis negat praesens tempus carere spatio, quia in puncto praeterit? sed tamen perdurat attentio, per quam pergat abesse quod aderit. non igitur longum tempus futurum, quod non est, sed longum futurum longa expectatio futuri est, neque longum praeteritum tempus, quod non est, sed longum praeteritum longa memoria praeteriti est.

134. See n. 112.

135. I have discussed the relations of Augustine to his predecessors more fully, *op. cit.* (in n. 111), pp. 162–171, 176–181, 184–187, 200–201. Some interesting paral-

lels between Augustine and Plotinus are pointed out by O'Connell, *op. cit.* (in n. 100), pp. 355–358. The extensive literature on this subject includes J. Guitton, *Le temps et l'éternité chez Plotin et saint Augustin* (Paris, 1933); J.-M. Le Blond, *Les conversions de saint Augustin* (Paris, 1950), pp. 246–275.

136. Nietzsche, e.g., in the first chapter of his *Philosophie im tragischen Zeitalter der Griechen* (*Philosophy in the Tragic Age of the Greeks,* ed. M. Cowan [Chicago, 1962], p. 31), says that the Greeks invented *"the archetypes of philosophic thought.* All posterity has not made an essential contribution to them since." J. Burnet, *Early Greek Philosophy* [4] (London, 1930), p. v, describes science as "thinking about the world in the Greek way."

Index

(See also, especially for Augustine, the table of contents.)

Aeschylus 7

Ambrose of Milan 23, 53, 54, 57, 61, 66, 68, 69, 71, 102, 103, 107

Anaxagoras 28, 30

Anselm of Canterbury 1–5, 15, 21, 32–39, 43–47, 96, 97, 104, 105

Aristotle 11, 19, 27, 28, 30, 48, 75, 76, 78, 82–85, 87, 88, 112–114

Audet, Th.-A. 96, 102, 105

Balthasar, H. von 112

Basil of Caesarea 81, 86, 112–114

Boethius 97, 98

Bogliolo, L. 111

Bonaventure 46

Bourke, V. J. 102

Bréhier, E. 97

Bröcker, W. 113

Burnet, J. 115

Callahan, J. F. 99, 112–114

Chrysippus 78

Clark, G. H. 112

Courcelle, P. 53, 63, 66, 68, 69, 106, 107, 109

Daniélou, J. 109

Descartes, R. 46

Diogenes Laertius 111

Dodds, E. R. 105

Dörrie, H. 107

Draeseke, J. 97, 98

Ecclesiastes 80

Empedocles 49

Epicurus 111

Eunomius 86

Euripides 8

Exodus 11, 18, 99

Gaunilo 43, 45, 46

Gibb, J. 97

Gilson, E. 46, 96, 99, 103, 104

Gregory of Nyssa 11–19, 21–23, 26, 30–33, 37, 39, 40, 55–58, 62–73, 77–81, 90–93, 100–104, 109, 112
Guitton, J. 115
Havelock, E. A. 107
Henry, P. 52, 53, 58, 73, 110
Heraclitus 6, 7, 10, 40
Hilary of Poitiers 102
Homer 5, 7, 10, 27, 29, 48, 52, 100
Horace 98, 106
Jaeger, W. 100, 103, 105, 106, 109
Kant, I. 1, 46
Le Blond, J.-M. 115
Manichaeans 22–25, 40
Merki, H. 104
Montgomery, W. 97
Moses 18
Nebridius 23, 25
Nietzsche, F. 115
O'Connell, R. J. 110, 111, 115
Orphics 48–51, 105
Parmenides 8–10, 12, 13, 15, 19, 30, 38, 39, 45, 98, 99, 107
Paul, St. 57, 74, 99, 107
Pindar 49
Plato 8–13, 15–19, 21, 26–28, 30, 31, 39–41, 49–51, 56, 58, 64, 67, 68, 72, 75–78, 90, 91, 98, 100, 105, 106, 112
Plotinus 11, 12, 14, 15, 19, 21, 23, 26–28, 31, 39, 51–54, 56–58, 61, 63–69, 71–74, 76–79, 89–92, 106–112, 115
Porphyry 107, 109
Psalms 107, 110
Pseudo-Dionysius 20
Pythagoreans 49, 51
Seneca 98
Sextus Empiricus 48, 82–84, 88, 105, 113
Socrates 50, 106
Stoics 28, 78, 100
Theiler, W. 107
Thomas Aquinas 15, 20, 32, 42–44, 46, 99, 102, 103
Varro 16
Wolff, C. 104
Woodbury, L. 98
Xenophanes 7–10, 13, 16, 18, 19, 26, 27, 30, 38, 98, 100
Xenophon 105

117

THE SAINT AUGUSTINE LECTURES

VILLANOVA UNIVERSITY

VILLANOVA, PA.

1959   *Saint Augustine on Personality,* by Paul Henry,
        S.J., Institut Catholique, Paris; New York,
        The Macmillan Company, 1960.

1960   *Platonism and Augustinianism,* by Raymond
        Klibansky, McGill University; unpublished.

1961   *Charter of Christendom: the Significance of the
        City of God,* by John O'Meara, University
        College, Dublin; New York, The Macmillan
        Company, 1961.

1962   *At the Origins of the Thomistic Notion of Man,*
        by Anton Pegis, Pontifical Institute of Medi-
        aeval Studies, Toronto; New York, The
        Macmillan Company, 1963.

1963   *Augustine's View of Reality,* by Vernon J.
        Bourke, St. Louis University; Villanova,
        Villanova Press, 1964.

1965   *The Resurrection and Saint Augustine's The-
        ology of Human Values,* by Henri I. Mar-
        rou, University of Paris; Villanova, Villa-
        nova University Press, 1967.

1966   *Saint Augustine and Christian Platonism,* A.
        Hilary Armstrong, University of Liverpool;
        Villanova, Villanova University Press, 1967.